COMPREHENSIVE MARITIME SECURITY IN THE INDIAN OCEAN REGION

COMPREHENSIVE MARITIME SECURITY IN THE INDIAN OCEAN REGION

Challenges and Opportunities

Edited by

Sithara Fernando

General Sir John Kotelawala Defence University (KDU)

Sri Lanka

in association with

KNOWLEDGE WORLD

KW Publishers Pvt Ltd
New Delhi

General Sir John Kotelawala Defence University (KDU) was initially established as the "General Sir John Kotelawala Defence Academy" by the Parliamentary Act No 68 of 1981 and subsequently it was elevated to University status by the amendment Act No 27 of 1988, thereby empowering it to award Bachelors' and Postgraduate degrees in Defence Studies.

KDU is a member of the Association of Commonwealth Universities (United Kingdom) and maintains necessary standards for educating and grooming Officer Cadets to meet the challenges of modern defence management.

KDU is now open for civil students who wish to continue their higher studies in the fields of Engineering, Law, Management, Social Sciences and IT.

Officers with exceptional performance in reputed universities/institutions can pursue postgraduate studies in accordance with the requirements of the Service to which they belong. Civil professionals are also offered a place at postgraduate studies to excel in and study a post graduate degree in their related field of expertise.

General Sir John Kotelawala Defence University (KDU) is one of the most prestigious defence universities in the South Asian region. The university offers academic opportunities for local and international students ranging from Bachelor's degree level up to PhD in Defence and Strategic Studies, Medicine, Engineering, Management, Law, Social Sciences and Humanities, Allied Health Sciences, Computing and Built Environment and Spatial Sciences. KDU is catering to both military and non-military higher educational demands. The KDU main university has its own Southern Campus at Hambantota, down south in Sri Lanka. The state of the art KDU hospital is also nearing completion in close proximity to the main university. This unique university has been a major breakthrough in tertiary education in Sri Lanka and in the region. KDU has now firmly established its identity as a leading international university in the region.

ISBN 978-93-89137-41-5 Hardback
ISBN 978-93-89137-42-2 ebook

KNOWLEDGE WORLD

KW Publishers Pvt Ltd
4676/21, First Floor, Ansari Road
Daryaganj, New Delhi 110002
Phone: +91 11 23263498/43528107
Marketing: kw@kwpub.com
Editorial: production@kwpub.com
Website: www.kwpub.com

Printed and Bound in India

Contents

Contributors

Mr. Mahinda Attanayake, BSc (Engineering), PGDPM, CPEng, MIPENZ, C.Eng. MIE (Sri Lanka), is a New Zealand professional who migrated from Sri Lanka more than thirty five years ago. He is a chartered professional engineer and a member of the Institution of Professional Engineers New Zealand and the Institution of Engineers Sri Lanka. He started his engineering career at Ceylon Steel Corporation and served as the Assistant Engineering Superintendent at Zambia Consolidated Copper Mines Limited in the Mufulira Mines in Zambia for several years before migrating to New Zealand. Currently, he is a Senior Projects Engineer at Watercare Services Limited in New Zealand. As a well-known social activist among the Sri Lankan community in Auckland, New Zealand, he has taken a keen interest in economic and social developments in Sri Lanka in the last two decades. Recently, he was instrumental in initiating a project to promote rainwater for the benefit of the rural population in the North Central province of Sri Lanka which is suffering from chronic kidney disease. He has edited several Newsletters in New Zealand and has authored numerous articles on key political and social issues in Sri Lanka, New Zealand and Australia. He is the current President of the New Zealand Society for Peace Unity and Human Rights in Sri Lanka (SPURNZ) and a past president of the Auckland Branch of United Sri Lanka Association.

Admiral (Dr.) Jayanath Colombage is a former chief of Sri Lanka navy who retired after an active service of 37 years as a four-star Admiral. He is a highly decorated officer for gallantry and distinguished service. He is a graduate of Defence Services Staff College in India and Royal College of Defence Studies, United Kingdom. He holds a PhD from General Sir John Kotelawala Defence University. He also holds a MSc in Defence and Strategic Studies from Madras University and a MA in International

Studies from King's College, London. He is a maritime security practitioner/specialist with wide experiences in countering maritime terrorism. He is a visiting lecturer at the University of Colombo, Defence Services Command and Staff College (Sri Lanka), Kotelawala Defence University, Bandaranaike Center for International Studies and Bandaranaike International Diplomatic Training Institute. He is a former Chairman of the Sri Lanka Shipping Corporation and a former adviser to the President of Sri Lanka on maritime affairs. He is a Fellow of Nautical Institute, London, United Kingdom. Admiral Colombage is currently the Director of the Centre for Indo-Lanka Initiatives of the Pathfinder Foundation. He is also a member of the Advisory Council of the 'Institute of National Security Studies Sri Lanka' and a Guest Professor at Sichuan University in China.

Dr. Sithara Fernando is a Senior Lecturer in the Department of Strategic Studies, Faculty of Defence and Strategic Studies, General Sir John Kotelawala Defence University (KDU), Sri Lanka. He has also been a Visiting Lecturer at the Department of International Relations, University of Colombo, Sri Lanka. He obtained his BSc in International Relations from the London School of Economics and Political Science, University of London, and his MA, MPhil and PhD from Jawaharlal Nehru University, New Delhi. He has also graduated twice from the College of Security Studies, Daniel K. Inouye Asia Pacific Center for Security Studies (DKI-APCSS), Hawaii, United States of America. He was also awarded the Symposium on East Asia Security (SEAS) Fellowship by the US Embassy in Sri Lanka for participating in the Advanced Security Cooperation Course at DKI-APCSS from September-October 2015. He is also a recipient of the Kodikara Award given by the Regional Centre for Strategic Studies (RCSS), Colombo, Sri Lanka. He has also been a visiting scholar at the Institute of Chinese Studies (ICS), Delhi. He has published two books, 'China's Maritime Relations with South Asia: from Confrontation to Cooperation' (Lambert Academic Publishing, Saarbrucken) and the 'United States-China-India Strategic Triangle in the Indian Ocean Region: Challenges and Opportunities' (editor, Knowledge World Publishers, New Delhi). He has also published a monograph, 'Maritime Cooperation in South Asia' (RCSS,

Colombo and Manohar, New Delhi), in the RCSS Policy Studies series. He has also published articles in the refereed journals 'China Report', 'Strategic Analysis' and 'Insight on Africa'. His 2014 Fellows Project Research Paper, 'The Contribution of the Galle Dialogue to Maritime Security Cooperation: Present Status and Future Possibilities' was published online by DKI-APCSS in their 'Alumni Perspectives' publication stream. He has also published two 'Occasional Papers' for Institute of Chinese Studies, 'China's Relations with the Indian Ocean Region: Combining Realist and Constructivist Perspectives', and 'China and the Cooperative Architecture in the South China Sea: Prospects and Problems'. He teaches International Relations, Strategic Studies and Maritime Security.

Colonel Saman Jayawickrama is a commissioned officer in the Sri Lanka Army posted to the Corps of Signals and currently serving at the Regimental Headquarters of the Corps of Sri Lanka Army Signals. His academic accomplishments span over Diplomas from national, Commonwealth International, postgraduate and masters with areas of interests ranging from general management , defense management , human resource management, conflict resolution and peace/reconciliation, youth in development and international relations and diplomacy. Col. Jayawickrama is basically a researcher in conflict/peace and regional studies in South Asia. He is a Master's degree holder in Management (Defense studies) from KDU, Master of Arts (MA)in International Relations from University of Colombo, Diploma in Conflict resolution from Bandaranaike Centre for International studies and Commonwealth International diploma in Youth in Development from Open University—Sri Lanka. He is currently a faculty member of the Institute of Personnel Management of Sri Lanka—IPM. During his 26 years of service in the Sri Lanka Army as a Signal Officer, he gained hands-on skills/experience in Satellite Communications and Cyber warfare on the combat communication domain, especially during the natural disaster situations in the Asia-Pacific Region while gaining overseas trainings and advanced qualifications on Geographic information system and remote sensing from University of Peradeniya—Sri Lanka. However, throughout his tenure in the Sri Lanka Army, six years of his unblemished service (from

2009–2015) as the Coordinating Officer and Staff Officer (Operations and Administration) to the Office of Strategic Affairs of the Ministry of Defense is the most remarkable period where he was able to practice the full force of his acquired synergy in a semi-military environment. Being an ardent researcher, Col. Jayawickrama has presented and published researches and study papers in both local/international academic forums. Individual paper presented in 2014 at the University of Colombo (available on the web ref: irofsrilanka2014@gmail.com) on South Asia's Regional Cooperation/ Integration on Energy Security at the International Conference on 'Sri Lanka in World Affairs' and South Asia's Regional Integration and Trade Agreements on Economic Security at Annual Symposium of KDU in 2015 are two such very informative pieces of his work. Over the above he carried out researches on 'Political Violence in the South in Sri Lanka', 'Impacts of illegal migration on states and human rights issues', 'Promotion of Regional Security in South Asia over the Role of SAARC', 'Contemporary Peace Building Initiatives with reference to constitutional attempts to resolve Armed Conflict in Sri Lanka', 'Rethinking the nexus between youth, unemployment and conflict perspectives from Sri Lanka' and 'Political violence against elected governments and its impacts on Societies' are just to mention few of what he has written so far. Col. Jayawickrama is currently reading for his MPhil/PhD from General Sir John Kotelawala Defence University—Sri Lanka.

Dr. Prabhakaran Paleri is the former director general of Indian Coast Guard with naval and marine customs background. Post retirement, he is engaged in research, academics and corporate governance. He is a speaker and also a visual media discussant. Professionally he has been trained by the Indian Navy and the United States Coast Guard. Academically he is a graduate in mechanical engineering with nuclear engineering as elective, postgraduate in business administration and a fellow in shipping management. He holds a Master's degree in national security strategy from the National Defense University, Washington, D.C. where he was inducted into the Hall of Fame in 2009. He holds a PhD degree in business administration and defence and strategic studies from the University of Madras. He has researched and authored ten books on strategic and management subjects and published various papers. In 2014, he attended the Annual Research Conference at General Sir John Kotelawala Defence University, Sri Lanka as a research presenter on 'Sea level Rise and Geoproperty Issues.' He has been awarded with the first Coast Guard Medal, commendation from the Central Board of Excise and Customs and the President's Coast Guard Medal for exemplary operational command and leadership while in active service. He lives in Kozhikode, Kerala, India. His areas of research interest are national security strategy, governance and ocean regimes besides his favourite 'Investing Capital Human' which he considers the next level in human resource management. He can be contacted on *ppaleri@hotmail.com.*

Commander Lanka Prasada (retired) is a retired naval officer, currently involved in academic research in the Faculty of Management Studies and Commerce, in University of Sri Jayewardenepura, focusing on interagency collaboration in public organisations. He has presented academic research papers on interagency collaborative capacity, focusing on law enforcement perspective of marine environment protection in Sri Lanka, at the International Conference on Business Management organised by Faculty of Management Studies and Commerce, of University of Sri Jayewardenepura, held in 2014 and 2015. His academic qualifications include, Master of Business Administration, Postgraduate Diploma in Management, Executive Diploma in Business Administration, and Postgraduate Diploma in International Relations—in which he won the Best Research Thesis Award. During his career of 20 years in Sri Lanka Navy, he has commanded several commissioned ships and establishments of the navy and actively taken part in many naval and amphibious operations. He won the Sword of Honour for the Best All-round Cadet, and later graduated top of the course in International Principal Warfare Officers' Course in School of Maritime Operations of Royal Navy, UK and Hydrography Specialisation Course in Indian Naval Hydrographic School. He played a key role in establishing the newly enacted Sri Lanka Coast Guard, and held the appointment of Director Operations at Coast Guard Headquarters. He has served in several interagency public committees inclusive of National Task Force on

Bay of Bengal Large Marine Ecosystem Project (BOBLME), Advisory Committee on Trafficking of Persons—Ministry of Justice and Committee on Enforcement—National Dangerous Drugs Control Board.

Dr. SinhaRaja Tammita-Delgoda, historian, art historian and writer, is well known as an authority on the art and culture of Sri Lanka. His 1st book, *A Travellers History of India* (UK, USA, 1994), is now in its 4th edition worldwide. One of the few non-combatants to have been allowed in the war zone during the final stages of the Eelam War, he has lectured on Insurgency and Terrorism in the United Kingdom, Canada and India, at the Royal Military Academy Sandhurst (RMAS) and the Centre for Land Warfare Studies (CLAWS), New Delhi, among other venues. From 2010-2015, he was Visiting Lecturer and Dissertation Supervisor at the Bandaranaike Centre of International Studies, Colombo (BCIS), specialising in South Asian Studies. His recent work has focused on the Indian Ocean, its geopolitics and its environment. In 2012, his essay titled 'The Kalpitiya Peninsula. A Unique Eco-System', was published in the 'Quarterly Journal of the India International Centre'. His study on trade, connectivity, shipping and politics in the Indian Ocean, 'A Key to the Future: Commonality, Divergence and the Path to Convergence' was published by the Indian Council on World Affairs in 'Transforming South Asia: Imperatives for Action' (2013). His latest work, 'A Hub for Disaster Relief in the Indian Ocean. The Case for Sri Lanka' (2015), was launched at the 1st ever International Disaster Convention, Colombo.

Commodore R. S. Vasan is currently the Director of the Chennai Centre of China Studies, Head, Strategy and Security Studies at the Center for Asia Studies and the Director of the Asian Secretariat of the World Borderpol. An alumnus of the Defence Services Staff College, College of Naval Warfare (CNW) and the International Visitor Leadership Programme, he has a distinguished service of over 34 years in the Indian Navy and the Coast Guard. His appointments include command of warships, two naval air stations and a long-range Maritime Air Squadron. His shore appointments include, Chief Staff Officer Operations, Regional

Commander of the Eastern Region of the Coast Guard, Instructor at the Naval War College and Director of Naval Aviation Staff. His additional assignments include, Member Advisory Group at the Madras University and Stella Maris College. He is also a visiting faculty at the Indian Maritime University, Hindustan Institute of Engineering, Academy of Maritime Education and Training and the Great Lake Institute of Management. He has been contributing to websites, journals, newspapers and also interacts with the media on a regular basis. He is a regular speaker at many international and national institutions and universities. He was also the Chairman of the Aeronautical Society of India, President of the Navy Foundation in Chennai and the Director at Tamil Nadu Ex-Servicemen Corporation (TEXCO), a Tamil Nadu Government-run organisation for ex-Servicemen. He is also invited regularly by national and regional Television to be on the panel on various discussions.

Mr. Ananda Weerasinghe, BA Honours (Cey), MPhil (Cantab), is a retired senior professional of the Sri Lanka Administrative Service (SLAS) now living in New Zealand. During his 30-year career with the government of Sri Lanka, he has held a number of senior positions in the land resources management sector. His interest in resource management led him to secure an Food and Agriculture Organization (FAO)-funded scholarship to pursue postgraduate studies in Land Economics at the University of Cambridge. He has the rare distinction of serving in Sri Lanka's national civil service as well as in the Foreign Service. Hand-picked by the Foreign Affairs Ministry, he served in the rank of Minister at the Sri Lanka's Mission to the European Union and the Embassy of Sri Lanka in Brussels, Belgium. He has been an extraordinarily talented student with a wide variety of interests and has the distinction of coming First-in-the-Island in two highly competitive public examinations in Sri Lanka. He was awarded the University Entrance Scholarship by the University of Ceylon, Peradeniya, for standing first at the University Entrance Examination. He repeated the feat by securing the first place at the Open Competitive Examination and interview process for the recruitment to the Sri Lanka Administrative Service (SLAS). He is the author of some academic papers on policy formulation and practices relating to agricultural settlements in Sri Lanka and currently serves in the Editorial Committee of the New Zealand Society for Peace Unity and Human Rights in Sri Lanka (SPURNZ).

1. Introduction

Admiral (Dr.) Jayanath Colombage

The ocean covers 71 percent of the earth's surface and contains 97 percent of the planet's water. The oceans have been playing a key role in the world for spreading civilisations, cultures, religions and affect the climate as well as weather. Humankind has been using the oceans since times immemorial for exploration, navigation, wars, trade, leisure and for obtaining many living as well as non-living resources. The ocean has been the main protein supplier for humankind. With the gradual increase of populations and the depletion of land-based resources, many countries are now focusing even more attention on the oceans. The oceans have been the lifeline of many countries and the economic live wire as well. There is a growing awareness in the world today regarding the exploitation of the ocean-based economy, which we need to be very careful about, as we cannot afford to damage the very ocean that is our lifeline. This new area of focus is termed as 'blue economy'. Blue economy refers to a sustainable ocean-based economic model that is largely dependent on coastal as well as marine ecosystems and resources. It is one that employs environmentally sound and innovative infrastructure, technologies and practices, including institutional and financing arrangements for meeting the goals of sustainable and inclusive development while protecting our coasts and oceans. The ocean is also considered as the last frontier in the search for novel drugs from nature to cure serious human diseases such as cancer, acquired immune deficiency syndrome (AIDS), tuberculosis and drug-resistant infections.

The Indian and Pacific Oceans are playing a significant role in world affairs in trade, economics, political and strategic areas in the 21st century. The Indian Ocean (IO) is fast becoming the key ocean in this century and this fact is clearly evident from the superpower attention being given to this ocean. "A Cooperative Strategy for 21st Century Seapower" has been published jointly by the world's sole superpower, America's sea services, the

US Navy, the Coast Guard and Marine Corps which speaks about their focus on the Indian and Pacific oceans in this century. This document has even divided the area into Indo, Asia and Pacific.[1] Similarly, an Australian white paper also talks about the growing prosperity and the economic as well as security significance of the Indian Ocean. Meanwhile, Japan, South Korea and Association of Southeast Asian Nations (ASEAN) countries also have realised the importance of the IO. The biggest resident power in the IO, India has naturally asserted its intentions by developing naval power projection capabilities in the region. China, which is fast becoming a new economic giant, has indicated her intentions to use the IO very clearly. All these factors provide a clear indication that IO has assumed great significance in world affairs in this century.

The IO features some of the busiest and key strategic shipping routes serving as a conduit for maritime trade between Asia, Persian Gulf, Africa, Europe and the Americas. The energy requirements of many nations depend on the IO as the fuel required by many industrialised nations is transported through it. It is also reported that 50 percent of the world's container traffic passes across the IO. This trade includes manufactured products, raw materials and commodities as well as development of trade centres, industrial zones, which in turn create jobs and opportunities. Ports also generate supporting activities, such as transportation, services and construction. This IO is a warm water ocean and experiences two well-established monsoons. The warm waters mean a rich diversity of fish as well as the availability to operate throughout the year and the monsoon brings in the rain thus, cooling the climate. The IO boasts of some of the world's largest fishing grounds, providing approximately 15 percent of earth's known catch.

There is an inevitable 'maritime cold war' brewing up in the IO and this ocean is becoming heavily militarised. The main spheres of influence in the IO are from United States of America, India and China. United

1. Department of the Navy, United States Marine Corps, Department of the Navy, United States of America, and the United States Coast Guard, "A Cooperative Strategy for 21st Century Seapower, 2015," https://www.uscg.mil/seniorleadership/DOCS/CS21R_Final.pdf, accessed on September 15, 2016.

States of America, being the perceived global policemen, is in the IO with the intention of maintaining freedom of international commerce. India is located in the IO littoral and the most powerful country in terms of naval and economic power. China is not located in the IO but depends heavily on it to obtain her energy and raw material requirements from the Middle East and Africa and to move her productions to the Middle East and Europe. The Sri Lankan Prime Minister while addressing the IO Conference held in Singapore in 2016, described this situation in the IO in the following manner: "growing militarisation, historical disputes and strategic mistrust pose serious challenges to the emergence of a viable and sustainable strategic security order".[2] It can be seen that the littorals of the IO and the major maritime users need to determine their own future rather than allowing this ocean to be manipulated by major powers for their own gains. These countries should play a more effective role in trade dynamics of the region without allowing any single state to dominate the system.

The IO has been vulnerable for various nefarious acts of non-state actors (NSAs). These NSAs can be in the form of terrorist groups, extremist ideologists, insurgents, pirates, smugglers of people, weapons and goods, and illegal, unreported and unregulated (IUU) fishing culprits. Hence, any security architecture in this ocean has to address these threat perceptions as well. IO is also home to some nuclear powers and proliferation of weapons of mass destruction (WMDs) is another concern. In this backdrop, this edited book titled 'Comprehensive Maritime Security in the Indian Ocean Region (IOR): Challenges and Opportunities' is very appropriate.

Eminent scholars and researchers from countries in the South Asian region have contributed some good articles adding to the academic discourse on the subject area. In chapter two, Dr. SinhaRaja Tammita-Delgoda looks at the marine environment as a geopolitical tool. He points out that Sri Lanka being an island nation has a unique, diverse and interesting marine environment and a significant location in the IO, and should assert its due

2. Hon. Ranil Wickremesinghe, 'Global Power Transition and the Indian Ocean', *Inaugural address by the Prime Minister of Sri Lanka at the Indian Ocean Conference on 1st Sep 2016 in Singapore,* http://www.pmoffice.gov.lk/download/press/D00000000050_EN.pdf?p=7, accessed on September 15, 2016.

position and ensure that this marine ecosystem is protected for the sake of the country's future. In chapter three, Commander (retired) Lanka Prasad pays special attention to 'Maritime Border Protection in Palk Bay and Palk Strait'. He speaks about the narrow body of water between southern India and northern Sri Lanka, the bilateral agreements and how the issue of poaching and bottom trawling by Indian fishermen has not been amicably resolved due to different perceptions of both the countries. He discusses not only the traditional security issues arising out of this situation but also the human security issues affecting the ordinary fishermen from Northern Sri Lanka. He also proposes some physical barriers as a measure to prevent Indian fishing trawlers poaching in large numbers in Sri Lankan waters. In chapter four, Commodore (retired) R.S. Vasan speaks about the Indian viewpoint on the Indo-Sri Lanka fishery conflict. His article is titled as 'Fisheries, Livelihood and Security in Palk Bay'. He speaks about the bilateral agreements for establishing the International Maritime Boundary Line (IMBL) and how the area was exploited by the Liberation Tigers of Tamil Eelam (LTTE). He blames the Tamil Nadu fishermen for not heeding any advice and for politicising the issue. He also talks about recent diplomatic initiatives aimed at finding a lasting solution to this issue and recommends a joint mechanism for investigating, patrolling and discussions at all levels to resolve this conflict. Dr. Prabakaran Paleri presents his findings in chapter five as 'Examining the Fisheries Issues at the Maritime Boundary Between India-Pakistan and India-Bangladesh'. He argues that marine fisheries can cause geostrategic issues impacting on the national security of involved countries. He recommends that the countries in South Asia should assume a different role and should safeguard the interests of all countries by preparing to meet challenges in the IO by eliminating conflict and maintaining tranquillity jointly, indifferent to their geopolitical differences for their common good. Colonel Saman Jayawickrama provides the Sri Lankan perspective of seaborne illegal migration from South Asia to Australia in chapter six. He speaks about the various trends and causes for irregular migration and various push and pull factors for the same. He emphasizes the need for maintaining a socio-economic balance in the country as a remedy to prevent irregular migration by sea. In chapter seven, Mr. Ananda Weerasinghe and Mr. Mahinda Attanayake provide an analysis of the response by Australia to irregular migration by sea. They speak about the increase of 'boat people' to Australia and their response to curb the menace. They argue that there should be more regional cooperation to prevent irregular migration by sea and all source countries have a role to play with a view of creating collective security and freedom from fear in the IO.

This edited volume by Dr. Sithara Fernando contains discussions on some very relevant and contemporary issues pertaining to comprehensive maritime security in the IO. The contents will be very useful to policymakers, researchers and maritime security practitioners alike. These papers enlighten the reader especially about key nontraditional maritime security issues. This awareness could assist in understanding various aspects in maritime security and maritime domain awareness in the IO. This understanding is necessary so as to maintain the required level of comprehensive maritime security and the sustainable use of this ocean for the betterment of the IOR.

Bibliography

Department of the Navy, United States Marine Corps, Department of the Navy, United States of America, and the United States Coast Guard, "A Cooperative Strategy for 21st Century Seapower, 2015," https://www.uscg.mil/seniorleadership/DOCS/CS21R_Final.pdf, accessed on September 15, 2016.

Hon. Ranil Wickremesinghe, 'Global Power Transition and the Indian Ocean', *Inaugural address by the Prime Minister of Sri Lanka at the Indian Ocean Conference on 1st Sep 2016 in Singapore,* http://www.pmoffice.gov.lk/download/press/D00000000050_EN.pdf?p=7, accessed on September 15, 2016.

2. Sri Lanka and the Sea

The Environment as a Geopolitical Tool[1]

SinhaRaja Tammita-Delgoda

What is an island? A body of land surrounded by water. Like the United Kingdom (UK) and Japan, Sri Lanka is a land mass surrounded by the sea. The sea therefore is its context. This is its environment. However, Sri Lanka has never really exploited its potential as an island. We have never really looked at it in this light before. As a result we have never really seen its context.

The case of Singapore presents a very interesting parallel. Located in the straits of Malacca between two land masses, Malaysia and Indonesia, Singapore in contrast has studied its context and charted its path accordingly. Using its position in one of the world's greatest shipping lanes and lifelines, it has used its geography to create its own environment. In the process it has become one of the busiest and most important ports in the world. This process has also seen Singapore become one of the richest countries in the world. In 2012, it was ranked the 3rd richest country in the world with an average per capita income of $56,694 a year.[2]

Sri Lanka occupies a very different position. Surrounded on three sides by the Indian Ocean, it has one of the most unique, diverse and interesting

1. This article is based on an address delivered at a Conference on "Sri Lanka's Ocean Resource: Our Hidden Gold Mine," Organized by the Lakshman Kadirgamar Institute of International Relations and Strategic Studies (LKIIRSS), Colombo, Sri Lanka. February 20, 2012.
2. *Forbes Magazine*, "In Pictures; The World's Richest Countries," (February 22, 2012). http://www.forbes.com/sites/bethgreenfield/2012/02/22/the-worlds-richest-countries/, accessed on January 10, 2013.

marine environments in South Asia. Trade is not its only option. When you are surrounded by the sea what do you do? You make use of it and what lies within it.

The sea is our environment. What lies in the sea belongs to us—it is a source of nutrition, income and livelihood. We must own it, we must use it and we must assert and defend our rights to it. An idea of the exclusive economic zone as defined by the Law of the sea gives us an idea of the potential. This is a vast space, where Sri Lanka can create its own vision, make a difference and set the tone.

Figure 2.1: Sri Lanka Territory and Exclusive Economic Zone (Survey Department of Sri Lanka, 1988)[3]

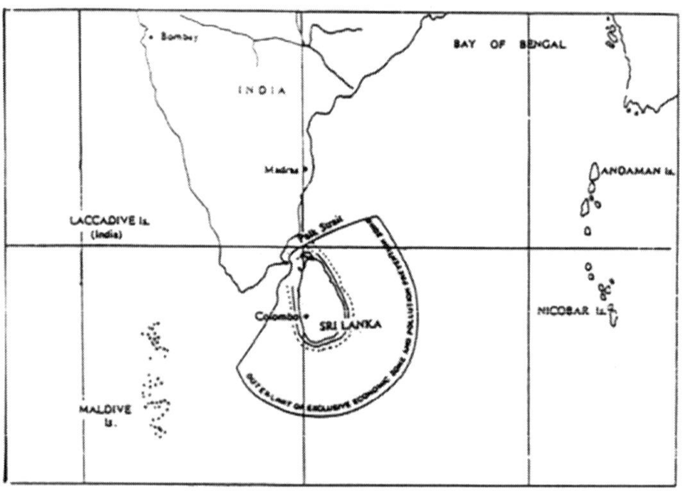

The seas to Sri Lanka's west, east and south provide one of the most diverse and interesting marine environments in South Asia. These seas house several living ecosystems and many rare and threatened species. They contain mangrove swamps and coral reefs. They are home to dugongs, whales and dolphins. These are all areas of international concern and have been the subject of international initiatives.

3. Case studies of the management of elasmobranch fisheries. Part 1, Management of Shark Fisheries in Sri Lanka, (Fisheries and Aquaculture Department) FAO. Corporate Document Depository http://www.fao.org/docrep/003/X2097E/X2097E15.htm, accessed on January 10, 2013.

Mammals, coral reefs, mangroves, tropical fish—have been viewed for a long time in a purely passive capacity as tourist attractions and sources of income, as things to be protected and conserved. However, they also have an important primary use which has not been tapped yet. Living things, living ecosystems, mammals, tropical fish, coral reefs all attract the attention of other living things, human beings. They move people, communities, countries and decision makers; they are a key to world opinion. As such they are dynamic levers and tools, with the power to influence and to shape. These levers can function as 'instruments' with the capacity to attract global interest and foster engagement worldwide. In short, they can serve as potent geopolitical tools. These tools may perhaps give Sri Lanka, the capacity and the capability which it badly needs at present, the ability to reach out and engage; to represent, to persuade and perhaps to influence.

Many of the ideas explored in this talk are the result of recent research conducted by products of the Bandaranaike Centre of International Studies (BCIS) and the Lakshman Kadirgamar Institute's Young Global Shapers Program. The principal influence has been the work of Shasheema Ambegoda on Sri Lanka and Public Diplomacy: The Art of Strategic Thinking and Communication (2012).[4] Ambegoda argues that environmental concerns transcend national boundaries, political divisions and geographical boundaries.[5] Like a tsunami or a typhoon, the negative impact of an environmental crisis has to be endured by all and often as not, it takes more than one country to tackle an environmental issue.[6] The purpose of environmental diplomacy[7] is to bring countries together on a common ground where they share a mutual interest, which at times can transcend all other concerns. In this field there are still opportunities and perhaps, compelling reasons to engage and reach mutual agreement.

4. Shasheema Ambegoda, "Sri Lanka and Public Diplomacy: The Art of Strategic Thinking and Communication" (PGD thesis, Bandaranaike Centre of International Studies (BCIS), 2012).
5. Ibid., p. 60.
6. Ibid.
7. Ibid., p. 59.

The conservation and management of natural resources is of utmost importance not just to one country or one region but for the global community as a whole. Obtaining international support to conserve Sri Lanka's natural resources and working in partnerships with governments and international organisations could prove very effective politically and diplomatically.[8] There is a potential to reach over the heads of hostile governments, to the general public of those countries. This could serve to offset the influence of hostile pressure groups and lobbies, such as the Liberation Tigers of Tamil Eelam (LTTE) diaspora in the west. At present, it is these pressure groups which hold the higher ground.

At the same time such avenues could lead to the strengthening of political ties with other governments. Negotiating treaties and agreements through bilateral or multilateral cooperation with states that have common environmental issues will help build relations and break new ground.[9] Environmental issues directly affect the health, safety and well-being of the world community.[10]Addressing them will gain attention.[11]

In the face of many crises which have all but overwhelmed it since the end of the Eelam War, Sri Lanka's diplomacy has tended to be reactive rather than proactive. This is one of the few areas left where Sri Lanka could take the initiative, where she can be proactive instead of reactive.

The largest Marine protected area on the island is the Bar Reef, a complex of reefs off the Kalpitiya peninsula on the north-western coast. Declared a marine sanctuary in 1992, this reef is one of Sri Lanka's great living treasures, her largest and perhaps her last pristine coral reef. These waters are home to more than 300 species of fish and they contain 138 varieties of stony coral.[12] The Bar Reef possesses the greatest biodiversity of any reef in South Asia. This gives it incomparable scientific value and it has immense environmental and economic significance for the whole region.[13]

8. Ibid., p. 77.
9. Ibid.
10. Ibid.
11. Ibid.
12. Arjan Rajasuriya, Marcus C. Ohman, M. W. Ranjith N. de Silva, "Coral Reefs of Sri Lanka: Human Disturbances and Management Issues," *Ambio: A Journal of the Human Environment*, vol. 24, no. 7–8, 1995.
13. Arjan Rajasuriya, Marcus C. Ohman, Olof Linden, "Human Disturbances on Coral Reefs in Sri Lanka. A Case Study," *Ambio* vol. 22, no. 7, 1993, p. 480.

The International Coral Reef Initiative (ICRI) describes itself as a partnership to preserve coral reefs and their related ecosystems around the world. Its partners are governments, international organisations and non-governmental organizations.[14] It was launched at the 1st Conference of the Parties of the Convention on Biological Diversity in December 1994, and at a meeting of the U.N. Commission on Sustainable Development in April 1995. The ICRI was originally initiated by the governments of Australia, France, Japan, Jamaica, the Philippines, Sweden, the United Kingdom and the United States of America.[15] In accordance with the United Nations Law of the Sea, it aimed to identify marine ecosystems exhibiting high levels of biodiversity as well as productivity and other critical habitat areas and provide necessary limitations on the use of these areas, through, inter alia, designation of protected areas.[16]

This section also went on to say that,

> Priority should be accorded to: Coral reef ecosystems, Estuaries, tropical wetlands, including mangroves, seagrass beds and other spawning and nursery areas.[17]

Since then the ICRI has been joined by many new partners, governments, United Nations organisations, multilateral development banks, environmental and developmental non-governmental organisations (NGOs). As a partnership, it has proved a potent instrument for international cooperation and collaboration. In 2012, the value and importance of the ICRI was acknowledged by the United Nations at the

---

Arjan Rajasuriya, Marcus C. Ohman, M. W. Ranjith N. de Silva, "Coral Reefs of Sri Lanka: Human Disturbances and Management Issues," *Ambio*, vol. 24, 1995, p. 434.

14. ICRI, International Coral Reef Initiative, "ICRI at a Glance," http://www.icriforum.org/about-icri, accessed on January 10, 2013.
15. Ibid.
16. International law, as reflected in the provisions of the *United Nations* Convention on the *Law of the Sea*, Report of UN Conference on Environment and Development (Rio de Janeiro, 3–14 June 1992), Chapter 17, Section 85, http://www.un.org/Depts/los/consultative_process/documents/A21-Ch17.htm, accessed on January 10, 2013.
17. Ibid.

67th session of the General Assembly. In a resolution titled 'Oceans and the Law of the Seas', the General Assembly declared that it reiterated its support.[18] This resolution was put forward by 45 countries, including the original founder members.[19]

The ICRI Secretariat is hosted by its members and rotates every 2 years.[20] Since 2004, this Secretariat has been co-chaired by a developed and a developing country, and at present the co-chairs are Belize and Australia. The potential for Sri Lanka is very clear, the format too seems ideal. Why not Kalpitiya? As the home of the Bar Reef, it seems a most logical place.

For the past few years, Sri Lanka has been locked in a long-bruising struggle against the United Nations Organisation. On one front it appears to be a struggle that she cannot afford to compromise on and cannot win, however, there are many other fronts on which Sri Lanka can perhaps engage, collaborate and make some headway. The United Nations Environment Programme (UNEP) is the body which coordinates the UN's environmental activities. Founded in 1972 as a result of the United Nations Conference on the Human Environment, its activities embrace the marine and terrestrial ecosystems. The UNEP has played a significant role in developing international campaigns and conventions. It has sponsored a number of successful projects, such as the preservation of marshlands in war-torn Iraq and declaration of the Year of the Dolphin in 2007. One of the projects to which the UNEP has given high priority is the implementation of the International Coral Reef Initiative.

In 1980, growing public concern caused the UNEP and the Food and Agricultural Organization (FAO) to draw up a global action plan for Marine Mammals Authorization Program (MMAP). This plan aimed

18. ICRI, International Coral Reef Initiative, "*ICRI Acknowledged by General Assembly,*" http://www.icriforum.org/news/2013/02/icri-acknowledged-united-nations-general-assembly, accessed on January 10, 2013.
19. Ibid.
20. ICRI, International Coral Reef Initiative, "*ICRI Secretariat,*" http://www.icriforum.org/about-icri, accessed on January 10, 2013.

to bring governments together to agree and harmonise their policies for marine mammal conservation. As the top level predators in the food chain, marine mammals have a tremendous impact on their ecosystems and are important indicators of the health of marine environments.

The UNEP is in the process of revising and updating its Global Plan of Action for Marine Mammals (MMAP). The current goal is to develop international treaties and conventions. These treaties and conventions serve as multilateral environmental agreements (MEAs) and they function as important vehicles and mediums. One of the most important of these is CITES—the Convention on International Trade in Endangered Species of Wild Fauna and Flora. Activated in 1975, CITES is an international agreement between governments.[21] The international trade in wild animals and plants, including fish and other marine life, is now a multi-billion-dollar business. It is crucial that such trade be managed in a sustainable and legal way. The aim of CITES is to ensure that international trade in specimens of wild animals and plants does not threaten their survival. An international treaty which now involves 177 governments, it is the conservation agreement with the largest number of members.[22]

CITES is widely recognised as one of the most effective and best-enforced international conservation agreements. Offering protection to more than 30,000 species around the globe, it has played a key role in preventing the extinction of numerous plants and animals.[23]

The Convention on the Conservation of Migratory Species of Wild Animals (CMS)[24] is another instrument which the UNEP relies heavily on. The CMS aims to conserve terrestrial, marine and avian migratory species throughout their range. Concluded under the aegis of the UNEP, it is an intergovernmental treaty concerned with the conservation of wildlife

21. Convention on International Trade in Endangered Species of Wild Fauna and Flora, "What is CITES?," http://www.cites.org/eng/disc/what.php, accessed on January 10, 2013.
22. Ibid.
23. Ibid.
24. Introduction to the Convention on Migratory Species, http://www.cms.int/about/intro.htm, accessed on January 10, 2013.

and habitats on a global scale. Since 1983, when it entered into force, its membership has grown steadily to include over 100 parties from Africa, Central and South America, Asia, Europe and Oceania.

Figure 2.2: Convention on the Conservation of Migratory Species of Wild Animals

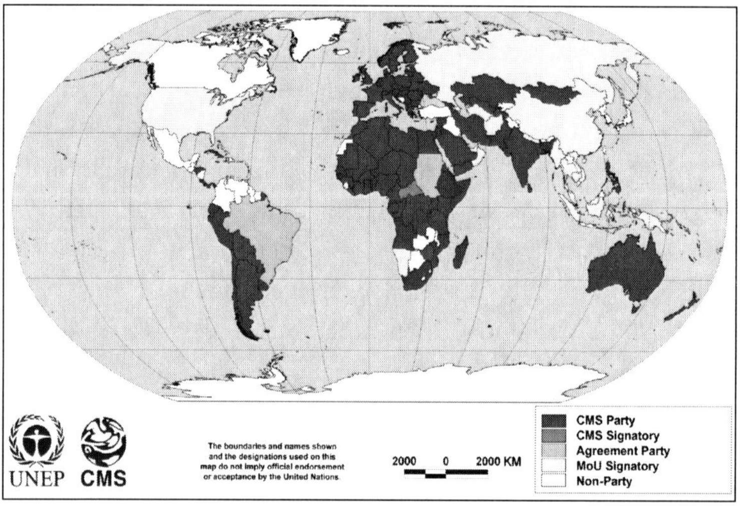

Source: http://www.cms.int/about/intro.htm

The CMS also applies to migratory birds and pelagic or ocean-going species. Every year Sri Lanka's coasts, wetlands and wildlife parks attract a vast variety of migrant species. What has not perhaps received as much publicity is that the island's marine environments also draw a range of sea-going and migrant species.[25] Nomads of the sea, these birds are found only in the deep sea and hardly ever come to the shore.[26] The Brown Noddy, for example, ranges right across the tropics, from the Red Sea to the Indian Ocean, the Pacific and the Caribbean.[27]

One of the rarest mammals on earth is the dugong. Often referred to as a sea cow, for thousands of years the dugong has been hunted for its

25. SinhaRaja Tammita-Delgoda, "Kalpitiya, The Sea, The Lagoon and the Islands," *India International Centre Quarterly*, Autumn, 2012, pp. 79–80.
26. Ibid.
27. Ibid.

meat and oil. Today it is an endangered species, close to extinction.[28] There are only a few places left in the world where the dugong can still be found. Sri Lanka is one of them and the Puttalam and the Mannar Lagoons are among the Dugong's last remaining footholds anywhere in the world.[29]

On January 31, 2012, Sri Lanka joined the international community to become a signatory to the Dugong Memorandum of Understanding (MOU).[30] Banning the hunting and selling of dugongs and their products, this MOU operates under the UNEP. This is one initiative where Sri Lanka could take the lead and inaugurate its own campaign. The dugong is so rare and unusual that any major program would be a path-breaking one. The successful implementation of such a program by a signatory would surely make global headlines.

Some of the most important forces deeply concerned with the marine environment are massive private institutions which in themselves represent deeply influential lobby groups. The Pew Charitable Trust, for example, is one of the richest and most influential private foundations in the United States of America. In 2009, its annual report valued its assets at $5.8 billion US. The trust also funds the Pew Research Center, the third-largest think tank in Washington DC, after the Brookings Institution and the Center for American Progress. Both these institutions are very well known worldwide and have considerable influence in the American foreign policy circles. The Pew Environment Group is the conservation arm of the Pew Charitable Trust. One of its declared aims is to save the marine environment and protect the rich array of life that it supports.

28. D. M. S. S. Karunarathna, M. A. S. Navaratne, W. P. N. Perera, V. A. P. Samarawickrama, "Conservation Status of the Globally Vulnerable Dugong (*Dugon dugon)* in the Coastal Waters of Kalpitiya Area in Sri Lanka," *Journal of Threatened Taxa,* vol. 3, no. 1, 2011, pp. 1485–1489; Anouk Ilangakoon, "Research and Conservation of Marine Mammals in relation to the Bar Reef Marine Sanctuary North Western Sri Lanka," prepared for The Coastal Conservation Department, Ministry of Fisheries and Ocean Resources, Sri Lanka and Asian Development Bank (August 2005).

29. Ibid.

30. Memorandum of Understanding on the Conservation and Management of Dugongs and Their Habitats throughout their Range, "Convention on Migratory Species (CMS)," http://www.cms.int/species/dugong/, accessed on January 10, 2013.

In the recent years, the Pew Environment Group has focused its attention on the conservation of the shark. Despite its well-established image as a predator, the shark plays an important role in maintaining the balance of the marine ecosystem. Sharks are vital for healthy oceans and habitats, such as coral reefs and seagrass beds. For more than 400 million years, they have helped regulate the variety and abundance of species below them in the food chain of the sea. Losing sharks could have consequences that affect the entire ocean ecosystem. It is something which the Pew Group has realised and made a priority.

The Pew Environment Group has identified the present moment as a critical time to reverse the global decline of shark populations. We will work internationally with our coalition allies to influence the fishing nations and treaty organisations that regulate high seas fisheries. In addition, we will work with nations whose waters still have diverse populations of sharks to declare shark sanctuaries and to advocate for international shark conservation.[31]

In line with this aim, the Pew Foundation has declared this year 2013 as its 'Year of the Shark'. It plans to put forward three proposals to protect the shark at the 16th meeting of the CITES on March 3–14, 2013, in Bangkok.

Sri Lanka has a large number of sharks in its marine waters. The whale shark is just one of them and it is has been sighted several times in the seas off Kalpitiya. However, the unregulated nature of shark fishing is a source of international concern and has already attracted the attention of the Pew campaign.

Recently, the group coordinated a meeting in Colombo to obtain further background for its proposals.[32] Included in the agenda was a trip

31. The Pew Charitable Trusts. Environmental Initiatives Campaigns, "Global Shark Conservation," http://www.pewenvironment.org/campaigns/global-shark-conservation/id/8589941059, accessed on January 10, 2013.

32. The Pew Charitable Trusts, Environmental Initiatives Campaigns, "Global Shark Conservation, Keri Lynn Miller, Dispatch from Sri Lanka: Observing the Trade of White Tipped Oceanic Sharks in a Local Fishmarket," February 8, 2013, http://www.pewenvironment.org/news-room/other-resources/dispatch-from-sri-lanka-observing-the-trade-of-oceanic-whitetip-sharks-in-a-local-fish-market-85899449974, accessed on January 10, 2013.

to the fish market in Negombo, one of the largest on the island, where several species of shark were on sale.[33] Among them was the White Tipped Oceanic Shark, one of the subjects of the proposed campaign.[34]

Dispatch from Sri Lanka

Observing the Trade of White Tipped Oceanic Sharks in a Local Fishmarket.

The countdown to the next CITES has begun. On a recent trip to Sri Lanka, Pew's Kerri Lynn Miller saw first-hand the need for the convention to protect shark and manta ray species.[35]

This is the type of campaign which Sri Lanka could and should support; not only is the island located near the area which has been earmarked for a sanctuary; but also the possibility of a massive and deeply influential institutional partner is ready and waiting.

Shark Habitats

Source: Pew Global Shark Conservation Campaign http://www.pewenvironment.org/newsroom/other-resources/the-truth-about-sharks-85899362412.

If initiatives like these are given the kind of support that they need, there is a good chance that they may succeed. If they do, Sri Lanka could well find herself at the heart of a massive international programme to save sharks. As the Pew campaign's headline says

33. Ibid.
34. Ibid.
35. Ibid.

"It's big business, it's big news, it's a big vote. Will 2013 be the 'Year of the Shark' at CITES."[36]

The benefits of such a programme are there for all to see. In July 2011, another island nation, the Bahamas joined the Maldives and Honduras in prohibiting the commercial fishing of sharks. The effect of this was to create almost 926,645 mi^2 of ocean, where these animals can now swim safely.

This action was so unusual and so spectacular that it caused international comment, even attracting the attention of the New York Times.[37] These are the words of the head of the Pew Global Shark Conservation:

Today's announcement permanently protects more than 40 shark species in Bahamian waters. We applaud the people and government of The Bahamas for being bold leaders in marine conservation.[38]

---

36. The Pew Charitable Trusts, Environmental Initiatives Campaigns, Global Shark Conservation, "It's Time to Protect Sharks and Manta Rays," February 28, 2013, http://www.pewenvironment.org/news-room/other-resources/its-time-to-protect-sharks-and-manta-rays-85899455290, accessed on January 10, 2013.
37. David Jolly, "Bahamas Bans Shark Fishing," *New York Times, Environment,* August 3, 2013 http://green.blogs.nytimes.com/2011/07/05/bahamas-bans-shark-fishing/, accessed on January 10, 2013.
38. "Bahamas Acts to Protect Sharks," The Pew Charitable Trusts. Environmental Initiatives Campaigns. Global Shark Conservation July 5, 2011, Press Release. http://www.pewenvironment.org/news-room/press-releases/bahamas-acts-to-protect-sharks-85899361467, accessed on January 10, 2013.

The Bahamian sanctuary was created by adding an amendment to the Fisheries Resources Act to prohibit commercial shark fishing along with the sale, importation and export of shark products. This is something which Sri Lanka can think of trying to emulate. Certainly it is something which will show the country in a positive light.

Protecting our marine species as part of an international conservation campaign will make it easier to protect our own fishing resources. It will garner sympathy and provide vital ammunition. This kind of participation will help Sri Lanka build a consensus against the Indian trawling fleets, which at present, it seems powerless to stop.

Between March and April 2011 the Sri Lankan Navy reported that more than 6,500 Indian trawlers had been spotted off the island's coasts.[39] It is also widely known that these trawlers employ a form of fishing which is banned in Sri Lanka—the use of large nets which sweep the ocean floor.[40] Sweeping up everything on the seabed, these nets not only trap all living organisms, but also trap the young fish.[41] Disrupting the breeding cycle, they threaten to deplete the ocean's marine resources.[42] For a country like Sri Lanka, the consequences could be disastrous. Not only does the fishing industry employ over 100,000 people, it feeds millions more.

The whole episode underlines how deeply interlinked the environment is with Sri Lanka's economic and national interest. Short of outright confrontation or abject appeasement, the only solution appears to be to harness international public opinion in a common cause.

Non-Alignment was a strategy which Jawaharlal Nehru perfected in the 1950s, when India was just emerging onto the world stage. Even if you are weak and poor, occupy the moral higher ground. It will enhance your profile, engender sympathy, provide vital ammunition and give you room to manoeuvre. As an issue of vital concern to everyone, the well-being of

---

39. Pia Chandavarkar, "Conflict brews between Sri Lankan and Indian fishermen," *BBC NEWS South Asia, Tamil Nadu* (April 7, 2011). http://www.bbc.co.uk/news/world-south-asia-12710928, accessed on January 10, 2013.
40. Ibid.
41. Ibid.
42. Ibid.

the environment cannot be ignored. An area where everyone has to be non-aligned—it offers a vital platform, a tool and perhaps a pulpit.

The only major initiative which Sri Lanka has produced on the management of natural resources is IOMAC, the Indian Ocean Marine Affairs Cooperation organisation. Formed in 1985 to bring about collective ocean management to the region, it included over several states from Indian Ocean and outside.[43]

IOMAC developed from informal consultations in the closing stages of the 3rd United Nations Conference on the Law of the Sea.[44] At the time many countries were slow to recognise that the mere assertion of their rights would not be enough. This alone would not bring the benefits which their vast sea areas and offshore potential entitled them to.[45] Several rounds of discussions underlined the need for a dedicated forum within which Indian Ocean marine affairs could be addressed and it was with this in mind that IOMAC was founded.

The purpose was threefold. The first was to create an awareness regarding the Indian Ocean and its potential among the states of the region.[46] The second objective was to provide a forum where Indian Ocean states and other interested nations could review the use of the Indian Ocean and identify fields in which they could benefit from cooperation, coordination and concerted action.[47] The third objective was to adopt a strategy for enhancing the national development of the Indian Ocean states through regular dialogue and the integration of ocean-related activities.[48]

During its time, IOMAC has launched several trailblazing measures, many of great environmental significance. Among the most significant

43. Cited in Ambegoda, "Sri Lanka and Public Diplomacy", pp. 60–62.
Hiran Jayewardena, "Indian Ocean Marine Affairs Cooperation (IOMAC)," in Peter Bautista Payoyo, ed., *Ocean Governance: Sustainable Development of the Seas* (Japan: United Nations University Press, 1994), http://archive.unu.edu/unupress/unupbooks/uu15oe/uu15oe0n.htm, accessed on January 10, 2013.
44. Hiran Jayewarden, "Indian Ocean Marine Affairs Cooperation (IOMAC)," http://archive.unu.edu/unupress/unupbooks/uu15oe/uu15oe0n.htm, accessed on January 10, 2013.
45. Ibid.
46. Ibid.
47. Ibid.
48. Ibid.

was the declaration in 1990 of the Indian Ocean as a 'A Sanctuary for Whales for All Time'.[49] Other groundbreaking initiatives have included 'the Banning of Large-scale Drift Nets' and the 'Initiation of Process Leading to the Establishment of an Indian Ocean Tuna Management' framework.[50]

Up till now, IOMAC has been the one and only Sri Lankan organisation to exploit Sri Lanka's unique position in the Indian Ocean. It is perhaps the only regional initiative of its kind to have originated in the United Nations Convention on the Law of the Sea (UNCLOS) process.[51] An initiative far ahead of it time, it was in many ways, perhaps too far ahead.

Since its inception, IOMAC has had to contend with fierce regional opposition. As a result it has been largely forgotten and marginalised in the greater scheme of things. Nevertheless, along the way, it has created a platform for the member states to foster significant political connections with influential international bodies and political figures.[52] While promoting cooperation among its member states and managing marine resources, IOMAC has also focused on regional cooperation forging intra-regional contacts. It has worked closely with a countless number of highly influential international organisations, such as the Asian-African Legal Consultative Committee (AALCC), Commonwealth Secretariat and the UNDP. These connections suggest the possibility of opening further doors to more opportunities in international politics.[53]

As a geopolitical tool, the potential of IOMAC is immense. This tool is still available to us and there is still time for Sri Lanka to utilise it. Perhaps the time has come to consider using something which was created by Sri Lanka, especially to serve its needs and safeguard its future.

The efforts of IOMAC to establish Sri Lanka as a regional hub are worthy of further study. It is unfortunate that there has only been one serious study to date of this pioneering initiative, which is Dr. Sithara

49. Cited in Ambegoda, "Sri Lanka and Public Diplomacy", p. 61.
50. Ibid.
51. Hiran Jayewarden, "Indian Ocean Marine Affairs Cooperation (IOMAC)".
52. Cited in Ambegoda, "Sri Lanka and Public Diplomacy", p. 62.
53. Ibid.

Fernando's article 'Co-operation in the Indian Ocean Region: Towards the Co-existence of IOMAC and IOR-ARC' published by the Australian research institute Future Directions International.[54] It is time for a substantial study of IOMAC. It is an example worth following and learning from.

The IOMAC Secretariat is the only one which is established in Colombo. Sri Lanka must aim to establish many more regional hubs in the field of conservation and environment. The geography of our position and the richness of our marine resources demand it. In this context, it is saddening to note that the regional headquarters of the world conservation body, the International Union for the Conservation of Nature (IUCN) has been shifted from Colombo to Bangkok. Sri Lanka has surely lost a major opportunity here.

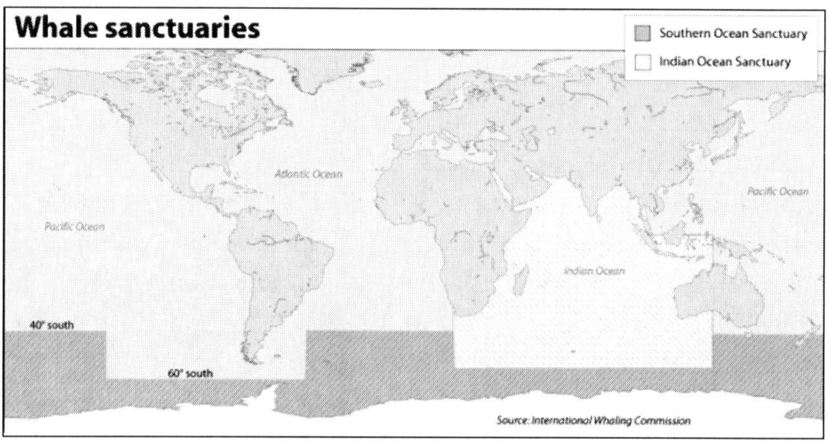

Whale sanctuaries in the Southern Ocean and Indian Ocean, Source: http://wwf.panda.org/?193865/Antarctic-whaling-ban-crucial-for-Southern-Hemisphere-whales

In 1979, the International Whaling Commission declared the Indian Ocean (north of 55°S) a sanctuary. The idea was advanced by another island

54. Y. J. Sithara N. Fernando, "Co-operation in the Indian Ocean Region: Towards the Co-existence of IOMAC and IOR-ARC," *Future Directions International, Associate Paper, Perth. Western Australia* (June 7, 2011). http://www.futuredirections.org.au/publications/associate-papers/84-associate-paper-co-operation-in-the-indian-ocean-region-towards , accessed on January 10, 2013.

nation, the Seychelles, with support from many Indian Ocean states, such as India, Kenya, Mauritius and Sri Lanka.[55]

The Indian Ocean has proved an important area for cetaceans, large and small. Unlike the Atlantic and Pacific Oceans, it has a northern coastline which prevents the migration of whales to Arctic waters. This could lead to the evolution of a unique population of whales.[56]

Sri Lanka stands at the very heart of the International Whaling Convention's Whaling Sanctuary. In the last few years it has gained international prominence for the richness and variety of its marine life, blue whales, killer whales and dolphins. A powerful vehicle, this opens yet another window for concerted action and cooperation.

In this context, the importance of doing research, encouraging research and making research facilities available should be a priority. Sri Lanka must reassess and reformulate its attitude to foreign research and foreign researchers. Research and publication are important global levers and we must be prepared to use them. It is significant that in the 2nd decade of the 21st century, only a limited amount of work has been done on Sri Lanka's marine environment. A series of seminal studies by Arjan Rajasuriya about Sri Lanka's coral reefs,[57] publications by Anouk Ilangakoon about Sri Lanka's whales and dolphins[58] and media programmes involving the blue whale, all these represent only the tip of what could and should be a mountain of serious scholarship by Sri Lankans. Without serious research of this kind, Sri Lanka cannot hope to establish itself as an environmental hub.

---

55. International Fund for Animal Welfare, "IFAW Summary Briefing: Indian Ocean Whale Sanctuary," http://www.ifaw.org/sites/default/files/Indian%20Ocean%20Whale%20Sanctuary.pdf, accessed on January 10, 2013.
56. Ibid., p. 1.
57. Arjan Rajasuriya, Marcus C. Ohman, M. W. Ranjith N. de Silva, "Coral Reefs of Sri Lanka: Human Disturbances and Management Issues," *Ambio: A Journal of the Human Environment,* vol. 24, no. 7–8, 1995.
   Arjan Rajasuriya, Marcus C. Ohman, Olof Linden, "Human Disturbances on Coral Reefs in Sri Lanka. A Case Study," *Ambio: A Journal of the Human Environment,* vol. 22, no. 7, 1993.
   Arjan Rajasuriya, Marcus C. Ohman, Ron Johnstone, "Coral and Sandstone Reefs in North Western Sri Lanka," *Hydrobiologia,* vol. 362, 1998.
58. Anouk Ilangakoon, *Whales & Dolphins of Sri Lanka* (Colombo: Wildlife Heritage Trust, 2002).

Sri Lanka cannot afford to leave this vital strategic option for Sri Lanka in the hands of purely local bodies, agencies and non-state players. The diplomatic service could act as a pivot which can function externally and deliver internally. Government should be engaging in international environmental fora through its diplomatic service. At the very least, it is important that Sri Lanka is represented. This is a battle Sri Lanka can win. If it does, it will become easier to fight the other battles. Do something really well, be recognised for it and it will provide a foundation on which to build.

Another institution which can be utilised is the Sri Lanka Navy. It is the one body in Sri Lanka with experience of the marine environment at many levels. It has trained personnel, infrastructure, seagoing craft and equipment. It also has a security interest to know what is happening in the seas around Sri Lanka.

The role played by the US Navy in the history of shark conservation and research in the 20th century provides an interesting parallel. The largest shark attack in recorded history occurred on July 30, 1945 when Japanese torpedoes struck and sunk the American Cruiser USS Indianapolis. The Indianapolis was the last major US Navy ship sunk by enemy action in World War II. Approximately 900 sailors donned live jackets and went into the sea. At sunrise the next day, the shark attacks began. The men were not rescued until five days later. By then, 579 men had died, an unknown number 'chewed to pieces' by sharks. The Discovery Channel in its programme 'Ocean of Fear', attributes the attacks to the oceanic white tip shark species. However, it also pointed out that most of the deaths were due to exposure, salt poisoning and thirst, with only the dead being dragged off by sharks.

Horrified by the episode, the US military invested massive sums in shark research and funded the search for a shark repellent. Research on sharks continues at The Naval Undersea Warfare Center, where it is highly classified. In a post-war era, monitoring, research and the conservation are all areas in which the Sri Lanka Navy could also find a new role. They could open up new avenues for the Sri Lanka Navy and its personnel. If nothing else, it will help create a new profile, add an extra dimension and open new windows.

The use of confidence-building measures (CBMs) plays an important role in the measures used to de-escalate tensions in conflict situations and build some kind of consensus which in turn could lead to cooperation. The capacity to work together towards a commonly desired goal creates the opportunity to build a relationship. The environment is a commonly desired goal. It can function as a platform—a confidence-building measure—which could be the beginning of a new positive perception which will associate Sri Lanka with very different things. To use marketing terms, it is in effect an exercise in rebranding, a change in the brand label. What does this do, it gives us a foundation on which to build a platform and a moral authority with which to speak.

In this context, successful campaigns to preserve our marine environment, if properly administered and fully implemented, can be very effective. They may give Sri Lanka the capability she needs to reach out and engage. When we engage, the lines are always open. It represents an opportunity for discussion, interaction and perhaps understanding on both sides.[59]

A cardinal principle of diplomacy is that if you cannot agree on the big things, maintain momentum by talking about other issues where you can agree.[60]

Upon winning the 2007 Nobel Peace Prize, former US Vice President Al Gore warned of the dangers of global warming.

We face a true planetary emergency. The climate crisis is not a political issue, it is a moral and spiritual challenge to all of humanity.[61]

Nature truly transcends all boundaries, like the tsunami, it reminds us that we are all similar. Surrounded as it is by the sea, Sri Lanka's marine environment could be a potent geopolitical tool. At a time when Sri Lanka appears to be becoming more and more isolated, the cause of the

59. Mr. Martin Moreland, November 2012. British Ambassador to Burma (1986), UK Permanent Representative to UN Geneva (1990).
60. Ibid.
61. Cited in, Ambegoda, "Sri Lanka and Public Diplomacy", p. 79.
NBC News, "Gore, U.N. climate panel win Nobel Peace Prize, Warming is 'greatest challenge' ever, he says, earning praise and criticism," October 12, 2007. http://www.nbcnews.com/id/21262661/ns/us_news-environment/t/gore-un-climate-panel-win-nobel-peace-prize/, accessed on January 10, 2013.

environment represents an instrument through which we can reach out in a common cause. Where we reach out in a common cause, we can engage.

The use of the environment as an arm of global politics is still not widely known. Environmental diplomacy "is, in fact, a concept that is so new, it has up to now gained acceptance only in very few, if any, ministries for foreign affairs around the world."[62] Over the last few years, Sri Lanka's collective morality, rightly or wrongly, has been called into question. Environmental diplomacy offers a way forward, an opportunity and a challenge, to change the way people see and think.

For an island nation, the preservation of its marine environment transcends issues like conservation, tourism and economics. It is much more than just a cause, it is a fundamental national interest.

Bibliography

Anouk Ilangakoon, *Research and Conservation of Marine Mammals in relation to the Bar Reef Marine Sanctuary North Western Sri Lanka,* prepared for The Coastal Conservation Department, Ministry of Fisheries and Ocean Resources, Sri Lanka and Asian Development Bank, August 2005.

Anouk Ilangakoon, *Whales & Dolphins of Sri Lanka* (Colombo: Wildlife Heritage Trust, 2002).

Arjan Rajasuriya, Marcus C. Ohman and M. W. Ranjith N. de Silva, "Coral Reefs of Sri Lanka: Human Disturbances and Management Issues," *Ambio: A Journal of the Human Environment,* vol. 24, no. 7–8, 1995.

Bahamas Acts to Protect Sharks, (July 5, 2011), Press Release, http://www.pewenvironment.org/news-room/press-releases/bahamas-acts-to-protect-sharks-85899361467, accessed on January 10, 2013.

Case Studies of the Management of Elasmobranch Fisheries. Part 1, Management of Shark Fisheries in Sri Lanka, Fisheries and Aquaculture Department, Food and Agriculture Organization (FAO), Corporate Document Depository. http://www.fao.org/docrep/003/X2097E/X2097E15.htm, accessed on January 10, 2013.

Convention on International Trade in Endangered Species of Wild Fauna and Flora (CITES), "What is CITES?," http://www.cites.org/eng/disc/what.php, accessed on January 10, 2013.

62. Cited in, Ambegoda, "Sri Lanka and Public Diplomacy", p. 59.
Lars Bjork Bom, "Resolution of Environmental Problems: The Use of Diplomacy," in John E. Carroll, ed., International Environmental Diplomacy, (USA: Cambridge University Press, 1988), p. 123, http://www.google.lk/webhp?ech=1&psi=SWmLUN6LBcrJrAfPyYDIBw.1351313743867.3&emsg=NCSR&noj=1&ei=SWmLUN6LBcrJrAfPyYDIBw, accessed on January 10, 2013.webhp?ech=1&psi=SWmLUN6LBcrJrAfPyYDIBw.1351313743867.3&emsg=NCSR&noj=1&ei=SWmLUN6LBcrJrAfPyYDIBw, accessed on January 10, 2013.

Convention on Migratory Species (CMS), "Introduction," http://www.cms.int/about/intro.htm.

D. M. S. S. Karunarathna, M. A. S. Navaratne, W. P. N. Perera and V. A. P. Samarawickrama, "Conservation Status of the Globally Vulnerable Dugong (Dugon dugon) in the Coastal Waters of Kalpitiya Area in Sri Lanka," *Journal of Threatened Taxa,* vol. 3, no. 1, 2011, pp. 1485–1489.

David Jolly, "Bahamas Bans Shark Fishing," *New York Times, Environment*, Saturday, (August 3, 2013), http://green.blogs.nytimes.com/2011/07/05/bahamas-bans-shark-fishing/, accessed on January 10, 2013.

Forbes Magazine, "In Pictures: The World's Richest Countries" (February 22, 2012). http://www.forbes.com/sites/bethgreenfield/2012/02/22/the-worlds-richest-countries/, accessed on January 10, 2013.

Hiran Jayewardena, "Indian Ocean Marine Affairs Cooperation(IOMAC)," in Peter Bautista Payoyo, ed., *Ocean Governance: Sustainable Development of the Seas* (Japan: United Nations University Press, 1994), http://archive.unu.edu/unupress/unupbooks/uu15oe/uu15oe0n.htm, accessed on January 10, 2013. http://www.futuredirections.org.au/publications/associate-papers/84-associate-paper-co-operation-in-the-indian-ocean-region-towards, accessed on January 10, 2013.

ICRI at a Glance, http://www.icriforum.org/about-icri, accessed on January 10, 2013.

ICRI Secretariat, http://www.icriforum.org/about-icri, accessed on January 10, 2013.

ICRI, "Acknowledged by General Assembly," http://www.icriforum.org/news/2013/02/icri-acknowledged-united-nations-general-assembly, accessed on January 10, 2013.

International Fund for Animal Welfare, "IFAW Summary Briefing: Indian Ocean Whale Sanctuary," http://www.ifaw.org/sites/default/files/Indian%20Ocean%20Whale%20Sanctuary.pdf.

International law, as reflected in the provisions of the *United Nations* Convention on the *Law of the Sea,* Report of UN Conference on Environment and Development (Rio de Janeiro, June 3–14, 1992), Chapter 17, Section 85, http://www.un.org/Depts/los/consultative_process/documents/A21-Ch17.htm, accessed on January 10, 2013.

"It's Time to Protect Sharks and Manta Rays" (February 28, 2013), http://www.pewenvironment.org/news-room/other-resources/its-time-to-protect-sharks-and-manta-rays-85899455290, accessed on January 10, 2013.

Keri Lynn Miller, "Dispatch from Sri Lanka: Observing the Trade of White Tipped Oceanic Sharks in a Local Fishmarket" (February 8 2013), http://www.pewenvironment.org/news-room/other-resources/dispatch-from-sri-lanka-observing-the-trade-of-oceanic-whitetip-sharks-in-a-local-fish-market-85899449974, accessed on January 10, 2013.

Malaka Rodrigo, "Sri Lanka signs International MOU to protect Dugongs," *Window to Nature.* http://window2nature.wordpress.com/2012/03/18/sri-lanka-signs-international-mou-to-protect-dugongs/, accessed on January 10, 2013.

Marcus C. Ohman and Olof Linden, "Human Disturbances on Coral Reefs in Sri Lanka: A Case Study," *Ambio,* vol. 22, no. 7, 1993.

Marcus C. Ohman and Ron Johnstone, "Coral and Sandstone Reefs in north western Sri Lanka, *Hydrobiologia,* vol. 362, 1998.

Memorandum of Understanding on the Conservation and Management of Dugongs and Their Habitats throughout their Range, Convention on Migratory Species (CMS). http://www.cms.int/species/dugong/, accessed on January 10, 2013.

Mr. Arjan Rajasuriya (IUCN), Colombo, Sri Lanka, in discussion with the author, October 2012.

Mr. Martin Moreland (British Ambassador to Burma (1986), UK Permanent Representative to the UN at Geneva (1990)), in discussion with the author, November 2012.

Pia Chandavarkar, "Conflict Brews between Sri Lankan and Indian Fishermen," BBC NEWS South Asia, Tamil Nadu (April 7, 2011). http://www.bbc.co.uk/news/world-south-asia-12710928, accessed on January 10, 2013.

Shasheema Ambegoda, "Sri Lanka and Public Diplomacy: The Art of Strategic Thinking and Communication" (PGD thesis, Bandaranaike Centre of International Studies (BCIS), 2012).

SinhaRaja Tammita-Delgoda "Kalpitiya, The Sea, The Lagoon and the Islands", IIC QUARTERLY, Autumn (New Delhi: India International Centre, 2012), pp. 67–81.

SinhaRaja Tammita-Delgoda, *The Sea, the Islands and the Lagoon, The Kalpitiya Peninsula*, Unpublished manuscript.

The Pew Charitable Trusts, "Environmental Initiatives Campaigns Global Shark Conservation," http://www.pewenvironment.org/campaigns/global-shark-conservation/id/8589941059, accessed on January 10, 2013.

Y. J. Sithara N. Fernando, "Co-operation in the Indian Ocean Region: Towards the Co-existence of IOMAC and IOR-ARC," *Future Directions International, Associate Paper, Perth. Western Australia* (June 7, 2011).

3. Maritime Border Protection in Palk Bay and Palk Strait

Lanka Prasada

Introduction

The waters between India and Sri Lanka in Palk Bay, Palk Strait and Gulf of Mannar are demarcated by the International Maritime Boundary Line (IMBL), which was ratified in 1974 and 1976, through bilateral agreements between the two countries. In the existing scenario, Indian trawlers from Tamil Nadu cross the IMBL in large numbers and fish in Sri Lankan waters illegally, utilising the banned fishing method of bottom-trawling. Similarly, there have been few occasions where Sri Lankan multi-day fishing boats have been arrested by Indian authorities for poaching in the exclusive economic zone (EEZ) of India. When encroaching Indian trawlers are apprehended by Sri Lanka Navy (SLN), the Indian fishermen make various allegations of harassment by SLN, which lead to protests of various forms in Tamil Nadu. This situation has recently flared up and developed into a political issue, and the State Government of Tamil Nadu has come up with various interpretations of certain clauses in the bilateral agreements of 1974 and 1976, and has called upon the Indian government to amend the bilateral agreements. The most famous claims made by politicians in Tamil Nadu are that the fishing community in Tamil Nadu is adversely affected due to the agreements, the IMBL should be redrawn, Katchatheevu Island should be restored to India and the bilateral agreements provide a right for Indian fishermen to engage in fishing in Sri Lankan waters.[1] This existing scenario has forced Sri Lankan authorities to adopt a soft policy towards Indian fishermen poaching in Sri Lankan waters, which place many constraints on maritime border protection and hamper

1. Government of Tamil Nadu 2012, Fisheries Policy Note 2012-2013, demand no. 7, Thiru K A Jayapal, Minister of Fisheries, Government of Tamil Nadu, pp. 17-18.

the law enforcement process against offenders, and exposes Sri Lanka to many political, economic, security, environmental and social ramifications. Though there were a myriad of strategies and bilateral discussions, no lasting solutions have been reached. This article examines various aspects related to the issue, which includes legal status and validity of interpretations in bilateral agreements, causes for intrusion and poaching by Indian fishermen and its consequences, existing status of poaching and maritime border protection in Sri Lankan waters, Indian perceptions and strategies, and options available for maritime border protection. The paper ends with conclusions derived on the examined aspects, and recommendations in the Sri Lankan context for enhancing maritime border protection as well as prevention of encroaching by Indian fishermen in Sri Lankan waters of Palk Bay and Palk Strait.

Interpretation of Legal Status in Bilateral Agreements on Maritime Boundary between Sri Lanka and India

This section contains discussion on the background of demarcating of maritime boundaries between two countries, bilateral agreements of 1974 and 1976 on the maritime boundary between Sri Lanka and India and the status of interpretations made on articles in two agreements.

Background of Demarcating the Maritime Boundary: Gulf of Mannar to Palk Strait

The first initiation of demarcating a maritime boundary between Sri Lanka and India in the historic waters from Palk Strait to Adam's Bridge goes back to the year 1920, where the governments of India and Ceylon accepted the desirability of demarcating a maritime boundary between two countries for the purpose of regulating fishing in Palk Bay and Palk Strait. The conference between delegations from the two countries on demarcating the maritime boundary had taken place on October 24, 1921 in Colombo, and the delegation from Ceylon had been led by Principal Collector of Customs Hon. B. Horsburg, who had earlier served as the Government Agent—Northern Province and had been knowledgeable about the fisheries issues in the region.[2]

2. Jayasinghe, Wijepala Tudor Jayasinghe, *Kachchativu and the Maritime Boundary of Sri Lanka* (Pannipitiya: Stamford Lake Publication, 2003), p. 13.

Even during this conference, the sovereignty of Katchatheevu Island had surfaced and the Indian delegation had proposed that the maritime boundary should be fixed one mile east of Katchatheevu and this would have placed Katchatheevu Island in Indian waters.[3] The delegation from Ceylon had rejected this claim while maintaining that Katchatheevu Island belongs to Ceylon and it was not a matter for negotiations as Ceylon had documentary proof for Ceylon's sovereignty of Katchatheevu Island, and the leader of Ceylon's delegation Mr. Horsburg had stated that the conference had to be dissolved, if the Indian delegation was disputing Ceylon's sovereignty of Katchatheevu Island.[4] The delegation from Ceylon had been very firm on Katchatheevu Island and finally, the Indian delegation had agreed to the maritime boundary proposed by the delegation from Ceylon. Then an agreement had been reached between the two delegations and both had agreed to the delimitation line, drawn three miles west of Katchatheevu Island, placing it well within Ceylon's territorial waters. Though not ratified by both countries, an agreement for the maritime boundary between two countries had been reached for the purpose of fisheries in October 1921.[5]

Agreement between Sri Lanka and India on the Maritime Boundary in Historic Waters of Two Countries in 1974

In the 1960s and 1970s, there had been a number of discussions between the officials of both governments to reach an agreement on the maritime boundary between Sri Lanka and India, and the dispute about ownership of Katchatheevu Island had delayed the agreement. The Indian government was adamant in having the Island in Indian territorial waters and shifting the boundary eastward of the Island. India's claim for sovereignty of the Katchatheevu Island was mainly based on an alleged title to the Island of the Rajah of Ramnad.[6] During the discussions, the officials from Sri Lanka had firmly held their ground and had refused to bow down to the pressure brought in by the Indian officials, stating that Sri Lanka's sovereignty over

3. Ibid., p. 15.
4. Ibid.
5. Ibid., pp. 15 & 132.
6. Jayasinghe, WT 2003, op. cit., p. 638.

Katchatheevu Island was not only based on historical documentary proof but also consistently exercising jurisdiction, control as well as the legislation for the Island.[7] Scrutinising details of the discussion held between the two delegations prior to signing the 1974 agreement, shows the standard of Sri Lankan diplomats and officials of that era as well as their firm stand, sound knowledge on the subject and concern of appropriate terminology. In one such situation, when the Indian delegation suggested that the Sri Lankan delegation could commence the discussion with 'claim' for the Katchatheevu island, the Sri Lankan delegation had objected to the word 'claim', stating that there was no question of Sri Lanka 'claiming' the Island, and if the Indian delegation is of the view that India has a 'claim', they are free to 'claim'.[8] The delegation from Sri Lanka had logically pointed out that it would not be appropriate for a country in that position of sovereignty to explain to another country, the foundations of its jurisdiction and control, and it would be more logical for a country which did not exercise jurisdiction and control to put forward their claim to the Island.[9] This incident shows the sharpness and alertness of the Sri Lankan officials of that era and, even a word that might have a slight impact on Sri Lanka's stand, was objected and corrected to ensure that Sri Lanka's stand was not weakened. Finally, the Indian officials had to agree to the Sri Lankan stand on the Katchatheevu Island. The demarcation of maritime boundary between Sri Lanka and India in the historic waters from Palk Strait to Adam's Bridge was formulated taking the 1921 agreement as the basis. Since the 1921 agreement had not been ratified by both governments, demarcation of the maritime boundary had been subjected to extensive negotiations, especially the distance from the boundary line to the Katchatheevu island. In accordance with the agreement formulated in 1921, the boundary line had been fixed, three nautical miles west of Katchatheevu island and India had been insisting on reducing the distance to 1/2 nautical mile—a stand opposed by Sri Lankan officials.[10] When the negotiations were deadlocked with both delegations not giving in, the officials had persuaded the two Prime Ministers to intervene to defuse

7. Ibid., p. 67.
8. Ibid., p. 66.
9. Ibid.
10. Ibid., p. 81.

the situation. The Prime Ministers, Mrs. Sirimavo Bandaranaike and Mrs. Indira Gandhi, who had a very cordial personal relationship between them, had consulted each other and finally come to a compromise and agreed to fix the boundary line one nautical mile west of Katchatheevu, which paved the way for signing of the bilateral agreement between Sri Lanka and India.[11] The formal bilateral agreement was signed by both countries in June 1974 and this provides the legal framework related to IMBL.

Significant Clauses in the Bilateral Agreement of 1974 and Interpretations

As per the international public law, an agreement on maritime boundaries reached by two states is internationally recognised and accepted, and binds all states. The significant clauses and the status of interpretations related to the agreement are indicated below.

The preamble to the agreement states that the boundary line and the related matters have been settled in a manner which is fair and equitable to both sides,[12] and confer sovereignty, exclusive jurisdiction and control over the own waters of the IMBL.[13] This preamble implies that both countries had accepted the fairness in the agreement and firmly close any ambiguity on bias towards one country.

The agreement provides provision, for Indian fishermen and pilgrims to visit Katchatheevu Island without travel documents and the vessels of both countries, the rights that they have traditionally enjoyed in each other's waters.[14] The politicians in Tamil Nadu interpret Article 6 as a right for Indian fishermen to fish in Sri Lankan waters. This article actually refers to the traditional navigation rights enjoyed by the fishermen and does not refer to fishing rights, and in fact none of the articles in the agreement refer to fishing rights. Even the Indian government's interpretation had been the same at the time of ratifying the agreement, and this is substantiated by the statement made by the then Minister of External Affairs of Indian government, Mr. Swaran Singh, at the Lok Sabha on July 23, 1974, which had

11. Jayasinghe, WT 2003, op. cit., pp. 91–93.
12. *Agreement between Sri Lanka and India on the boundary in historic waters between the two countries 1974*, Colombo, preamble.
13. Ibid., Article 4.
14. Ibid., Articles 5 & 6.

clarified the traditional rights as the traditional rights of the Indian fishermen and pilgrims to visit Katchatheevu island, and traditional navigation rights exercised by Indian and Sri Lankan vessels in each other's waters.[15] This statement strengthens the interpretation that traditional rights do not refer to fishing rights in Sri Lankan waters for Indian fishermen, but refers to the traditional rights of fishermen and pilgrims to visit Katchatheevu as well as traditional navigation rights of fishermen.

The 1976 Agreement between Sri Lanka and India on the Maritime Boundary

Both countries formulated and ratified another agreement on May 10, 1976, demarcating the maritime boundary between Sri Lanka and India in the Gulf of Mannar and the Bay of Bengal. This agreement, which extends the maritime boundary agreement of 1974, provides similar provisions as the 1974 agreement, with respect to sovereignty over the historic waters and territorial sea in IMBL's own side as well as the navigation rights.[16]

Significant Clauses in the Bilateral Agreement of 1976 and Interpretations

It provides sovereignty rights and exclusive jurisdiction over the EEZ and continental shelf as well as over living and non-living resources, falling on own side of the IMBL.[17] This article implies that Sri Lanka is vested with powers and authority to regulate fishing in its own waters.

There had been subsequent correspondence between the two countries with respect to the agreement, and one such correspondence states that "The fishing vessels and fishermen of India shall not engage in fishing in the historic waters, the territorial sea and EEZ of Sri Lanka nor shall fishing vessels and fishermen of Sri Lanka engage in fishing in the historic waters, the territorial sea and EEZ of India, without the express permission of Sri Lanka or India."[18] This clause also strengthens the interpretation that Indian fishermen do not have rights for fishing in Sri Lankan waters.

15. Jayasinghe, op. cit., pp. 100 & 101.
16. *Agreement between Sri Lanka and India on the maritime boundary between the two countries in the Gulf of Manaar and the Bay of Bengal 1976*, Colombo, Articles V1 & V3.
17. Ibid., Article V2.
18. Jayasinghe, op. cit., p. 141.

Existing Fishing Systems and Status of Marine Resources in Sri Lanka and India

This section contains fishing systems in Northern Province of Sri Lanka, fishing systems in Tamil Nadu and the existing status of living marine resources in Indian waters.

Fishing System in Northern and Eastern Provinces of Sri Lanka

The Department of Fisheries and Aquatic Resources (DFAR) is the legitimate regulatory authority for fisheries management in Sri Lanka and no person or vessel can engage in fishing in Sri Lankan waters without a valid licence issued by DFAR.[19] Since the DFAR does not issue licenses for trawling, it has become a prohibited fishing method in Sri Lankan waters. There are 26,000 fishing families and 9,475 registered boats of 18–28 ft in length with an outboard engine motor (OBM) in the Northern Province. They are traditional fishermen and not fishing entrepreneurs who use harmless fishing methods for fishing.[20]

Fishing System in State of Tamil Nadu

A fishing ban exists in Tamil Nadu from April 15 to May 30 every year, which is categorised as a fish-breeding period and also an Artisanal Fishing Zone of 3 nautical miles from the shore, exclusively for non-motorised fishing craft in India.[21] The state of Tamil Nadu has a large fishing fleet of 54,420, which includes 5,256 trawlers of varying sizes ranging from 50 to 70 feet in length, and they are large and rigid, in comparison to the Sri Lankan boats.[22] The fishing population in Tamil Nadu is about 860,000, comprising of 260,000 active fishermen. Most fishermen in Tamil Nadu are not boat-owners and work for wages; about 75

19. Sri Lanka Government 1996, *Fisheries & Aquatic Resources Act No 02*, Colombo, ss 6-14.
20. Proceedings of India-Sri Lanka the joint working group on fisheries, "Fishing within the Boundaries in Northern Waters of Sri Lanka," *Department of Fishery and Aquatic Resources (DFAR), Colombo, 2012.*
21. Pramod Ganapathiraju, *Illegal, Unreported and Unregulated Marine Fish Catches in the Indian Exclusive Economic Zone—Field Report* (Vancouver: MRAG, 2010), p. 24.
22. Pramod, Ganapathiraju, "Illegal and unreported fishing: global analyses of incentives and a case study estimating illegal and unreported catches from India" (PhD diss., University of British Columbia, 2012), p. 102.

percent of the boat-owners are non-fishing owners and 60 percent of the net income goes to the boat-owners, 40 percent to the fishermen-crew, and in certain cases, it is only daily wages and incentives, based on the weight of the catch.[23] This system of cash-incentives has led to quantity-based targets of fish caches, even through illegal fishing, to maximise their incentives.

Existing Status of Living Marine Resource Management in Indian Waters

The studies conducted on marine resources in Indian waters have revealed the following five factors which affect the management of living marine resources and contribute for the depletion of living marine resources.[24]

Overcapacity in mechanised fishing boats: The uncontrolled expansion of mechanised fishing fleet in India has resulted in overcapacity in the fishing fleet, over-exploitation and depletion of fish stocks in Indian waters. The collective mechanised fishing fleet in the coastal states of India is over 50,000 and the Marine Fishing Policy of India specifies the optimum fleet size of mechanised vessels as 15,998.[25] This shows a huge overcapacity and the appropriate fleet should only be 32 percent of the existing fleet. When this percentage is applied to Tamil Nadu trawler-fleet, it should be reduced to 1,682 from the present fleet of 5,256 trawlers, to bring the trawler-fleet to the optimum size.

Illegal Fishing during fish-breeding periods: The fishing-ban and fish-breeding period varies from state to state and when the ban is in force in one state, the trawlers from other states enter and fish in waters during the fishing-banned period.[26] This hampers fish-breeding, leading to depletion of fish stocks and the purpose of the declared fish-breading period is lost.

23. *Utopia*, "Palk Bay fishermen's plight and the need of the hour" (February 24, 2011), http://ameilie87.blogspot.com/2011/02/palk-bay-fishermens-plight-and-need-of.html, accessed on June 22, 2012.
24. Pramod, G. 2010, op. cit., p. 6.
25. Divya Varkey, Ganpathiraju Pramod, Tony Pitcher, "An Estimation of Compliance of the Fisheries of India with Article 7 (Fisheries Management) of the UN code of Conduct for Responsible Fishing, in *Fisheries Centre Research Reports* University of British Columbia, Canada, vol. 14, no. 2, accessed on June 10, 2012, pp. 1–24.
26. Pramod, G. 2010, op. cit., p. 7.

Illegal Fishing in artisanal zones: Due to depleted fish stocks in normal fishing grounds, mechanised trawlers invade into artisanal fishing zones and engage in illegal fishing, which hamper the recovery of fish population.[27]

Unregulated and improperly regulated fishing: There are unregulated and improperly regulated areas in the fishing system in India, such as absence of a common fishing-ban period for all the coastal states to protect fish-breeding periods,[28] and inconsistency in implementing a time-based programme to facilitate the conversion of mechanised trawlers to deep-sea fishing crafts as well as a gradual reduction of trawler-fleet in India to an established optimum level.

Ineffective monitoring, controlling and surveillance (MCS): The effectiveness of monitoring, controlling and surveillance mainly depends on the state of surveillance infrastructure and the effectiveness of enforcement mechanism. There are a myriad of laws, regulations and instructions issued by relevant authorities in India to facilitate the proper management of marine resources, which need to be implemented, monitored and controlled by the respective authorities. The assessment carried out on MCS in India has revealed that effectiveness is around 40 percent.[29]

Existing Status of Poaching by Indian Fishermen and Maritime Border Protection along IMBL

This section contains the distances involved in IMBL, the present system and extent of poaching by Indian fishermen, main poaching areas in Sri Lankan waters, existing status of sea patrols and responses of Indian fishermen, status of law enforcement against the poaching fishermen and practical constraints in maritime border protection.

IMBL between Sri Lanka and India in Palk Bay and Palk Strait

The bilateral agreement of 1974 demarcates IMBL from Talaimannar to Point Pedro. It is marked by six positions and the distances between two adjacent positions are indicated in order of the sequence in Table 3.1.

27. Ibid., p. 6.
28. Ibid.
29. Varkey, D., Pramod, G., & Pitcher, T., 2006, op. cit., p. 23.

Table 3.1: IMBL in Palk Bay and Palk Strait: segments and distances[30]

Segment No.	Area Covered by Two Points	Distance along IMBL
1	North of point Pedro to North of Kankasanthurai	14 Nautical Miles
2	North of Kankasanthurai to North-West of Karaitivu	30 Nautical Miles
3	North-West of Karaitivu to North-West of Delhi Island	20 Nautical Miles
4	North-West of Delft Island to South-West of Kachchativu	20 Nautical Miles
5	South-West of Kachchativu to Adam's Bridge (Talaimannar)	15 Nautical Miles
Total Distance along IMBL From Point Pedro to Talaimannar		99 Nautical Miles

Source: Author construction.

Chart 3.1: Poaching by Indian trawlers in waters of Sri Lanka—Jan 2006 to Jan 2009[31]

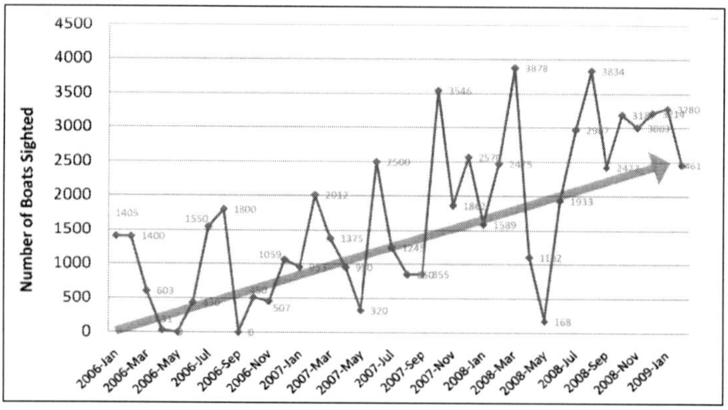

Source: Proceedings of India-Sri Lanka the joint working group on fisheries, 2012.

Present Extent of Poaching by Indian Fishermen in Sri Lankan Waters

Poaching in the waters between Sri Lanka and India around IMBL has existed for decades. The fishing ban imposed in Sri Lankan waters, by the government of Sri Lanka due to war, resulted in a gradual increase of poaching by Indian fishermen in Sri Lankan waters during the period

30. Admiralty Chart & Publications 1584: Trincomalee to Point Calimere, 2010.
31. Proceedings of India-Sri Lanka the joint working group on fisheries, 2012, op. cit.

from 2006 to 2009, as indicated in Chart 3.1. This trend still continues and the annual total of Indian fishing boats sighted poaching by sea patrols in Sri Lankan waters in the year 2011 was 45,656, and from January to October in 2012, a total of 43,737 trawlers have been sighted out of which, 4,571 trawlers had been identified by boat registration numbers.[32]

Poaching System of Indian Fishermen

The Indian trawlers generally encroach into the Sri Lankan waters three days a week, and the radar images of the whole poaching operation of Indian fishermen in Palk Bay and Palk Strait were monitored and recorded by SLN and are available with the DFAR. The Indian trawlers cross the IMBL in the evening, commence poaching with the nightfall and retreat to Indian waters in the early hours, and with this scenario, the waters of Sri Lanka are packed with Indian trawlers by midnight as shown in Figure 3.1. The poaching pattern clearly shows that poaching takes place very close to the Sri Lankan coast, which confirms that encroachments are not accidental, but intentional.

Figure 3.1: Encroaching by Indian Trawlers into Sri Lankan waters—situation in midnight[33]

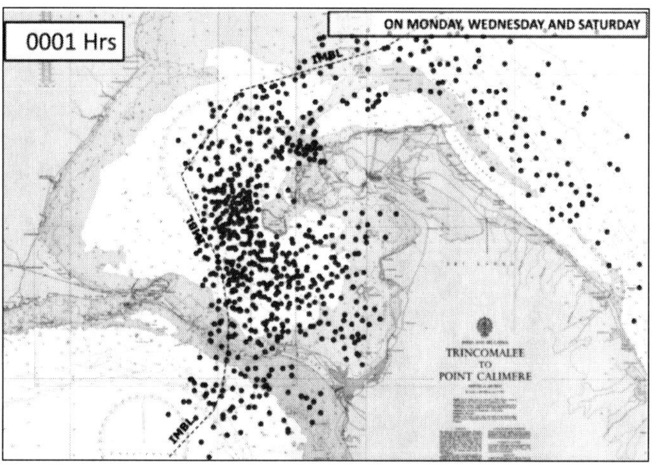

Source: Proceedings of India-Sri Lanka the joint working group on fisheries, 2012.

32. Proceedings of India-Sri Lanka the joint working group on fisheries, 2012, op. cit.
33. Ibid.

Main Poaching Areas in Waters of Sri Lanka

When the concentration of poaching by Indian fishermen is analysed, it shows three main poaching areas, as illustrated in Figure 3.2.

Poaching segment-PS1: The main concentration of poaching is in the area between Talaimannar, Katchatheevu and Delft Island, which extends up to the Sri Lankan coast. This area is the most critical segment as it is the richest area for prawns and the corresponding segments of IMBL for this area consist of segments 4 and 5 as indicated in Table 3.1, which extend to 35 nautical miles.

Poaching segment-PS2: The next concentration of poaching takes place in the sector encompassed by the area between north of Delft Island and west of Karaitivu, and up to Sri Lankan coast. This is the next prawns-rich area, and the corresponding segment of IMBL for this area consists of Segment 3 as indicated in Table 3.1, which extends to 20 nautical miles.

Poaching Segment-PS3: There is also less severe poaching concentration in area between Kankasanthurai to Point Pedro, extending up to IMBL, and the corresponding segments of IMBL consist of Segment 1 as indicated in Table 3.1, which extends to 14 nautical miles.

Figure 3.2: Identified main poaching concentrated segments in Sri Lankan waters[34]

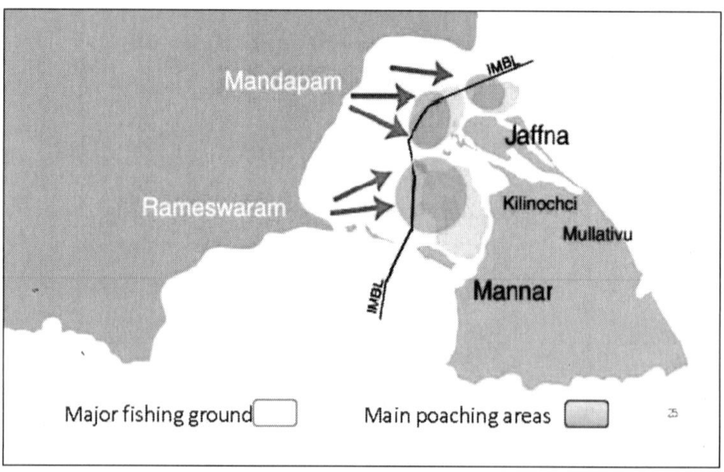

Source: Proceedings of India-Sri Lanka the joint working group on fisheries, 2012.

34. Proceedings of India-Sri Lanka the joint working group on fisheries, 2012, op. cit.

Existing Status of Sea Patrols by Border Protection Agencies of Sri Lanka and India

The Navies and Coast Guards of India and Sri Lanka carry out border patrols along IMBL in their own waters independently but joint-patrols or coordinated-patrols by two countries are not carried out. Though the patrols are carried out regularly, the statistics show that hundreds of Indian trawlers cross IMBL and poach in Sri Lankan waters regularly. This implies that deficiencies exist in sea patrols and border protection by both countries. Since the elimination of Liberation Tigers of Tamil Eelam (LTTE) in Sri Lanka, there is no major security threat to India from the Sri Lankan side and effective sea patrols along IMBL are greatly beneficial to Sri Lanka, than India.

Responses by Poaching Indian Fishermen to Sea Patrols of Sri Lanka

The sea patrols deployed by SLN and Sri Lanka Coast Guard (SLCG) frequently confront the encroaching Indian fishermen who cross the IMBL for poaching, and in such instances Indian fishermen claim that:

- they did not possess navigational aid to establish own location at sea and their entry into Sri Lankan waters was unintentional and accidental;
- IMBL is not marked physically and they were unaware of IMBL;
- personnel of SLN assault, harass, rob, and kill Indian fishermen;
- they were in Indian waters and SLN sea patrols entered Indian waters and attacked them.

Chart 3.2. Data of Sri Lankan fishermen arrested by Indian authorities 2008–2011[35]

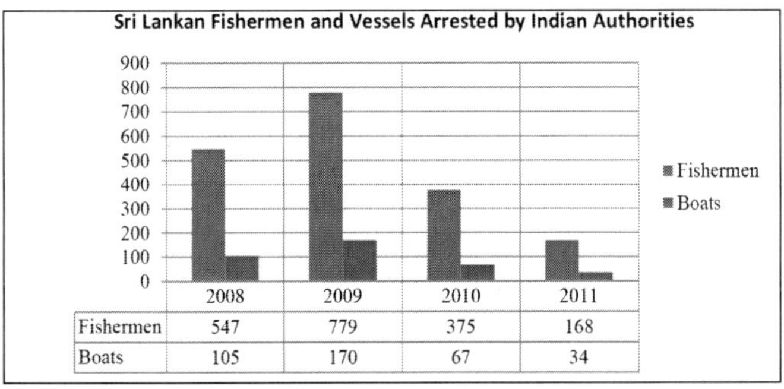

Source: Proceedings of India-Sri Lanka the joint working group on fisheries, 2012.

35. Proceedings of India-Sri Lanka the joint working group on fisheries, 2012, op. cit.

Status of Law Enforcement against Poaching Fishermen

The law enforcement process against poaching involves detection, apprehension, investigation, producing in judicial courts, prosecution, termination of the case, and it is revealed that two countries adopt two different approaches in legal processes.

Law Enforcement by Indian Authorities

When the Indian authorities apprehend Sri Lankan fishermen for fishing in EEZ of India, far away from Indian coast, Indian authorities initiate legal actions against them and details are illustrated in Chart 3.2. The Sri Lankan authorities have experienced many difficulties in getting Sri Lankan fishermen released, though the Indian fishermen arrested in Sri Lanka are released quickly.[36]

Law Enforcement by Sri Lankan Authorities

When SLN apprehends the Indian fishermen poaching in waters of Sri Lanka close to the Sri Lankan coast, it results in allegations against SLN and protests in Tamil Nadu. Then the Indian officials get involved, pressure is brought down on Sri Lankan authorities and the apprehended Indian fishermen are either released at magistrate courts or released without initiating any legal action. In the recent past, except for a few occasions, no legal actions have been initiated against Indian fishermen apprehended for poaching.[37]

Actual Ground Situation and Practical Constraints in Maritime Border Protection

Though many articles and reports have been written on maritime border protection, virtually none had given due considerations to practical constraints faced by sea patrols. The naval personnel who have experiences in sea patrols along the IMBL, especially in small and medium patrol crafts are aware of these constraints and personal experiences in such patrols reveals the following constraints:

36. Proceedings of India–Sri Lanka the joint working group on fisheries, 2012, op. cit.
37. Ibid.

The soft policy by the government of Sri Lanka towards Indian fishermen who poach, such as introduction of restrictions, limiting the scope of law enforcement actions of sea patrols, have made law enforcement at sea, a difficult task.

When Sri Lankan waters between the Sri Lankan coast and IMBL are congested with Indian trawlers, it is difficult for a few crafts of SLN and Coast Guard to match the intensity of encroachment and prevent encroachment.

During the decades of war, the Indian fishermen were afraid of poaching well within Sri Lankan waters due to the risk of misidentification for LTTE and getting attacked by SLN, as LTTE boats, including suicide boats operated in the area. Hence, the fear perception towards SLN sea patrols posed as a deterrent to encroaching Indian trawlers and on sighting the SLN patrol craft, would move away. With the termination of war and the soft law enforcement policy of Sri Lankan authorities, this deterrence has vanished, and Indian trawlers poach well within Sri Lankan waters disregarding the presence of SLN sea patrols, until physically stopped by SLN.

When a large number of Indian trawlers cross the IMBL simultaneously, the patrolling vessel has to proceed to hearing distance of each encroaching Indian trawler to warn. This is a time-consuming exercise, and when this endeavour with one Indian trawler takes place, dozens of other trawlers in the area around the patrol craft cross the IMBL, enter Sri Lankan waters, scatter in the area quickly and engage in poaching. Once they are scattered, it is practically impossible for the patrol craft to approach each and every trawler to warn and chase them away.

When a large number of Indian trawlers with dragging trawling nets operate in the night, it is difficult for the patrol craft to manoeuvre amongst large number of trawlers, as possibilities exist for the propellers of the craft to get entangled with fishing nets. In such situations, divers have to be called in to clear the propellers. Hence, SLN patrol crafts have to maneuver with great care when operating amongst large number of trawlers.

Political Ramifications and Consequences of Poaching by Indian Fishermen in Sri Lanka

This section commences with political ramifications on Sri Lanka, which includes Indian perception and thinking. Then it proceeds on to explain the economic and marine environmental consequences on Sri Lanka and ends with discussion on security as well as social consequences.

Indian Approach and Political Ramification for Sri Lanka

The Tamil Nadu government and the politicians in India never admit that Indian fishermen contravene applicable laws by poaching in Sri Lankan waters,and always make allegations of attacks by SLN. It is only the Indian Coast Guard (ICG), who has first-hand knowledge about the actual ground situation in Palk Bay and Palk Strait, and can take a different stand. The Deputy Director General of ICG making a statement at the Madras High Court, has dismissed the allegation that SLN vessels enter Indian waters and attack Indian fishermen, and has stated that 17,102 Indian fishing boats had poached in the Sri Lankan waters between June and October 2011.[38] The coalition government of India, sometimes bows down to the Tamil Nadu pressure and in the existing scenario, India-Sri Lanka Joint Working Group has been formed to address the fishery issue and the 4th meeting of the group was held in January 2012. The analyses of the joint statement of the meeting as reported by Asian Tribune website[39] reveals that India is not focusing on the prevention of poaching by Indian fishermen, not supporting Sri Lanka's stand on respecting the IMBL, not supporting the proposal for joint sea patrols by Navies and Coast Guards of the two countries and tries to promote some mechanism which would allow Indian fishermen to fish in Sri Lankan waters. India is emphasizing on the continuation of dialogue between fishermen's associations in India and Sri Lanka to find a solution. During such discussions between two associations, an agreement has to be reached between the two fishing associations, which

38. *The Hindu*, "State must also act to protect fishermen: Coast Guard" (November 17, 2011), *The National Aquatic Resources Research & Development Agency, no. 38.*

39. *Asian Tribune*, 2012, "4th meeting of the India–Sri Lanka Joint Working Group on Fisheries". http://www.asiantribune.com/news/2012/01/14/4th-meeting-india-sri-lanka-joint-working-group-fisheries, accessed on June 22, 2012.

suggests that permission be granted for Indian fishermen to fish in Sri Lankan waters up to 3 miles from the Sri Lankan coast for 12 hours a day and 70 days a year.[40] These proposals have no legitimate base and impracticable to enforce at sea, as enforcing actions at sea is highly complex, vastly different to enforcement actions on land, and persons who have experiences at sea would understand these difficulties. If such proposals are accepted, it would lead to uncontrolled invasions by Indian trawlers and ransacking of living marine resources in Sri Lankan waters, by a largely outnumbered Indian fishing fleet. This would also affect the sovereignty, territorial integrity, jurisdiction, security and safety of Sri Lanka, and ultimately result in political interference and more complicated ramifications involving two countries and clashes by two fishing communities.

Economic and Marine Environmental Consequences

The economic and marine environmental consequences caused due to poaching by Indian fishermen have been established by the Sri Lankan authority and a brief description is indicated below.

Economic Consequences

The Palk Bay and Palk Strait areas in Sri Lankan waters are relatively shallow and rich in prawns. When hundreds of Indian trawlers engage in poaching, it causes a vast economic loss. The DFAR of Sri Lanka has estimated Sri Lanka's annual economic loss due to poaching to be Rs. 8.6 billion annually.[41]

Marine Environmental Consequences

Bottom-trawling by Indian trawlers causes immense damage to the living and non-living marine resources. Bottom-trawling involves dragging the trawl net along the seabed as illustrated in Figure 3.3. The two heavy metal panels fixed at both sides of the mouth of the bottom-trawling net resembles a cowcatcher of a train, and they pick and crush everything at the sea bottom during dragging. The damages caused to the marine environment include the creatures at sea

40. V Vivekanandan, "Trawl Brawl," India—Sri Lanka Transborder Fishing, Samudra Report no. 57, November, 2010. p. 24.
41. Proceedings of India-Sri Lanka the joint working group on fisheries, 2012, op.cit

bottom, sea grass and corals and Figure 3.4 illustrates the damages caused to the marine environment by bottom trawling, which takes years for regrowth.

Figure 3.3: Bottom trawling—trawl net and features[42]

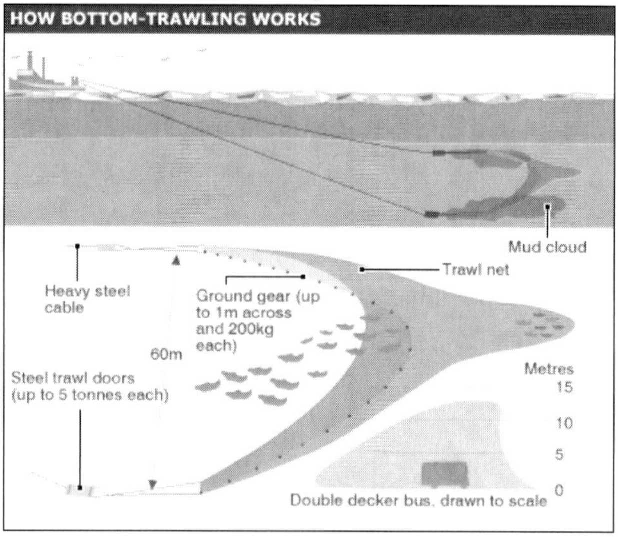

Source: Department of Fishery and Aquatic Resources (DFAR), 2012.

Figure 3.4: Marine environmental destruction caused by bottom trawling[43]

Picture: Before Trawling	**Picture: After Trawling**
	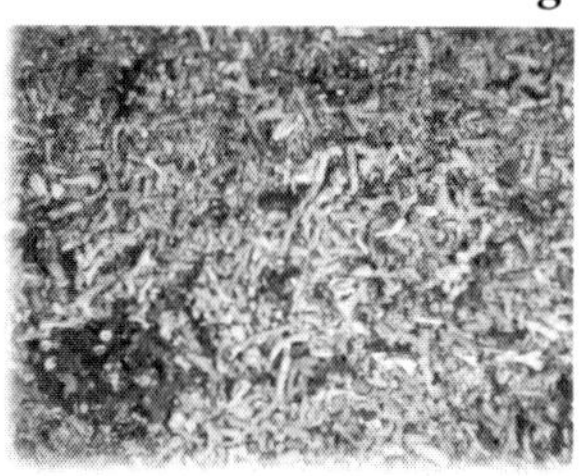

Source: Department of Fishery and Aquatic Resources (DFAR), 2012.

Security and Social Consequences

The repercussions of restrictions placed on the rightful law enforcement actions of Sri Lankan border protection agencies, against the poaching Indian fishermen

42. Proceedings of India–Sri Lanka the joint working group on fisheries, 2012, op. cit.
43. Ibid.

would not confine to fishing alone and would lead to following consequences:

- adverse short-term and long-term consequences on safety and security of the country in many spheres, such as transboundary movements of terrorists, criminals, illegal immigrants, human smuggling, weapons, explosives and narcotics;
- poaching by Indian fishermen leads to loss of livelihood of local fishermen, affecting the fishing community and it would develop into a socio-economic issue;
- the poaching Indian fishermen damage the fishing nets, boats and other fishing apparatus of Sri Lankan fishermen, placing financial burdens on them;
- The absence of effective law enforcement action by Sri Lankan authorities to prevent encroachment of Indian fishermen, would result in local fishermen taking law into their own hands and confronting Indian fishermen, which has happened recently. If this perpetuates, it would reach uncontrollable levels, making a huge security and political issue.

New Options Available for Maritime Border Protection

This section contains details of Vessel Monitoring Systems (VMS), identification of the IMBL at sea and Offshore security barriers available for maritime border security.

Vessel Monitoring System

The Vessel Monitoring System (VMS) consists of transmitters, Global Positioning System (GPS) satellites, VMS satellites, processing centre and monitoring as well as controlling centres. In these systems, transmitters of the VMS are required to be fitted onboard vessels and the position of vessels could be displayed in the VMS, as well as in processing centres and control stations, which can issue warnings to vessels. VMSs are active systems and movements of vessels are monitored through signals transmitted by vessels, and if the VMS transmitter onboard a vessel is switched off or disconnected, the position of the vessel cannot be obtained.

Options Available for Identification of IMBL

At present it is not possible to identify the limits of IMBL physically as it is not marked at sea. The charted depths of water along the IMBL in Palk Bay and Palk Strait range between 7–13 m and the nature of seabed is suitable for laying marker buoys. Hence marker buoys could be laid along IMBL. The other option is to utilise electronic charts with GPS systems in vessels and incorporate the coordinates (latitude and longitude) of the identified position along IMBL into the electronic charts. This would enable the boat operators to locate their own position as well as that of the IMBL. It has also been revealed that, if it is required to have a warning system with facilities to activate an alarm in boats as well as in controlling stations, that facility is also available for installation in Indian trawlers.[44]

Installing of Offshore Floating Barriers (OFBs)

One of the strategies available in maritime security spectrum is the utilisation of Offshore Floating Barriers (OFBs, which has not been experimented with in Sri Lanka, except for a limited usage in harbour defence system in harbour premises occupied by SLN.

Types of Organisations Involved in OFBs

There are two types of organisations involved in OFBs; one is the 'designing and consulting companies' and the other is 'manufacturing companies'. The designing and consulting companies conduct feasibility studies and design offshore barriers most suited for the specific situation. The manufacturing companies build various types of offshore barriers, based on their own designs or given designs and, some versions of offshore barriers are indicated below.

- Fixed Boat Barriers,
- offshore Floating Boat Barriers,
- line of Demarcation Barriers (LOD),
- anti-Terrorist Barriers,
- small Craft Intrusion Barriers.

44. K. Suresh Kumar and K. Sharath Kumar, "Design of Low Cost Maritime Boundary Identification Device using GPS System," *International Journal of Engineering Science and Technology* vol. 2, no. 9, pp. 4665–4672.

Features of OFBs

The OFBs have been designed and manufactured to meet varying ground situations, and some significant features in OFB systems are indicated below.[45]

- stop impacts of individual or multiple high-speed boats, safely and securely;
- prevent penetration by larger boats at lower speed;
- provide a clearly visible line of demarcation (deterrent effect);
- allow security forces to have a clear field of view through the barrier;
- designed to withstand varying wind, wave, and tidal forces;
- availability of built-in gates;
- high resistance to corrosion, ultraviolet (UV) degradation, low maintenance requirements/costs;
- fast and cost-effective installation;
- solar-powered lighting can be fixed to the barriers to facilitate identification in the night.

Design and Quality Assurance of OFBs

There are OFBs of varying designs and a few designs are illustrated in Figures 3.5–3.8. The OFB system consists of segments of rigidly built floats, which are interconnected with chains and each segment is anchored to the seabed. A brief description of OFB is indicated below.[46]

- The barriers are manufactured in segments of varying lengths from 15–100 m.
- Any number of segments can be connected to extend the total length of the barrier.
- Generally, each barrier segment of 100 m is anchored to the seabed, and the type of anchoring method as well as the distance between anchoring points depends on the sea conditions and type of the seabed in anchoring locations.
- The impact-withstand ability of the barriers have been tested through 'crash-tests' using boats with varying weights and speeds up to 40 knots.
- Barriers have been tested in offshore locations, such as oil rigs in mid-

45. A. G. Geobrugg, (n.d.) "Maritime Security Barriers," 2.102.04.EN.1101/1000, Romanshorn, Switzerland, www.geobrugg.com, accessed on February 25, 2011.
46. V-Navy, *Barriers at Sea, Levallois-Perret*, France, www.v-navy.com, accessed on February 25, 2011.

ocean in adverse weather conditions and have the ability to withstand heavy winds and rough weather.

- Barrier systems have been already installed in following non-friendly weather conditions:
  - water depths in excess of 68 m;
  - winds above 112 km/h;
  - prolonged winters with heavy icing and a large fluctuation in tides of more than 30 m.

Figure 3.5: FOXX floating boat barrier[47]

Source: Geobrugg AG (n.d), Maritime Security Barriers, 2011.

Figure 3.6: Line of demarcation (LOD) barrier in strong current and wind[48]

Source: V Group (2010), barriers at sea, 2011.

47. Geobrugg, A. G. n.d., op. cit.
48. V-Navy 2010, op. cit., pp. 1–16.

Figure 3.7: Anti-terrorist barrier in operation[49]

Source: V Group (2010), barriers at sea.

Figure 3.8: OFB in operation[50]

Source: V Group (2010), barriers at sea.

49. V-Navy 2010, op. cit., pp. 1–16.
50. Ibid.

Findings and Conclusions

The analyses of all relevant facts reveal that the maritime border protection between India and Sri Lanka in Palk Bay and Palk Strait focuses on two interlinked perspectives, namely, the Indian perspective and Sri Lankan perspective. Hence, the findings and conclusions are presented in this section focusing on two perspectives. This section commences with findings and conclusions on the legal status and interpretations of agreements, laws and regulations. The next paragraph contains a derived linked model of cause-problem-consequences, followed by the Indian perception and approach towards border protection and fisheries issues. The last sections deal with the repercussions of existing policies and the status of maritime border protection and evaluation on border protection options in Sri Lankan context.

Legal Status and Interpretations of Bilateral Agreements, International Conventions, Laws and Regulations

The analysis of bilateral agreements of 1974 and 1976 between India and Sri Lanka and other laws and regulations on fishing in waters of Sri Lanka reveal following findings and conclusions:

IMBL is an internationally accepted and recognised maritime border and Sri Lanka has the sovereignty, exclusive jurisdiction and control over the historic waters, internal waters and territorial sea of Sri Lanka and law of the country is applicable in these Sri Lankan waters.

Sri Lanka also has the legitimate right to promulgate laws and regulations with respect to management and conservation of marine resources in maritime zones of Sri Lanka, inclusive of regulations with respect to innocent passage. Hence, Sri Lanka has the right to proceed with law enforcement and legal process against Indian fishermen poaching in the waters of Sri Lanka.

SLN personnel above the rank of Petty Officer have the right to enforce fisheries laws and regulations of Sri Lanka and this provides legitimate authority for SLN to arrest Indian fishermen poaching in Sri Lankan waters.[51]

---

51. Sri Lanka Government 1996, *Fisheries & Aquatic Resources Act No 02*, Colombo, s 66.

Since Article 4 of the Bilateral Agreement of 1974 provides sovereignty, exclusive jurisdiction, and control over the waters falling on own side of the IMBL, Articles 5 and 6 should be read with Article 4.[52] When the articles are considered together, it implies that Indian fishermen have no right to fish in Sri Lankan waters. This stand is further strengthened by subsequent correspondence on agreements and the statement made by then Minister of External Affairs of Indian government in the Lok Sabha on July 23, 1974.[53] Hence, the claims made by Tamil Nadu politicians with respect to fishing rights for Indian fishermen in Sri Lankan waters have no legitimate validity.

India and Sri Lanka government have not ratified the agreement reached between the fisheries associations of the two countries. The clauses in this agreement, which affect the territorial integrity of Sri Lanka, are clearly not within the mandate of fisheries associations, and the agreement they have reached has no legal basis, legitimate validity or recognition.

Causes for Encroachment and Poaching by Indian Trawlers

Generally, every problem has causes for the problem and consequences of the problem. In certain interlinked situations, the problems and consequences of one situation become the causes and problem, respectively, for the other linked situation. The previous discussions reveal that causes for poaching by Indian fishermen could be developed as a 'cause-problem-consequences' model with two interlinked scopes, Sri Lankan context and Indian context, as illustrated in Figure 3.9.

Indian Perspective

This paragraph explains the Indian perspective of the maritime border protection in Palk Bay and Palk Strait. The paragraph commences with the Indian perception and approach on border protection, followed by the problem and the causes for the problem in Indian perspective and ends with the consequences of the problem.

52. *Agreement between Sri Lanka and India on the boundary in historic waters between the two countries 1974*, op. cit., s 4, 5 & 6
53. Jayasinghe 2003, op. cit., p. 101.

Indian Perception and Approach on Border Protection and Fisheries Issues

This sub-paragraph focuses on Indian perception and approach in two levels; the perception and approach of Indian government and the state government of Tamil Nadu.

Figure 3.9: Interlinked model of causes-problem-consequences developed through findings

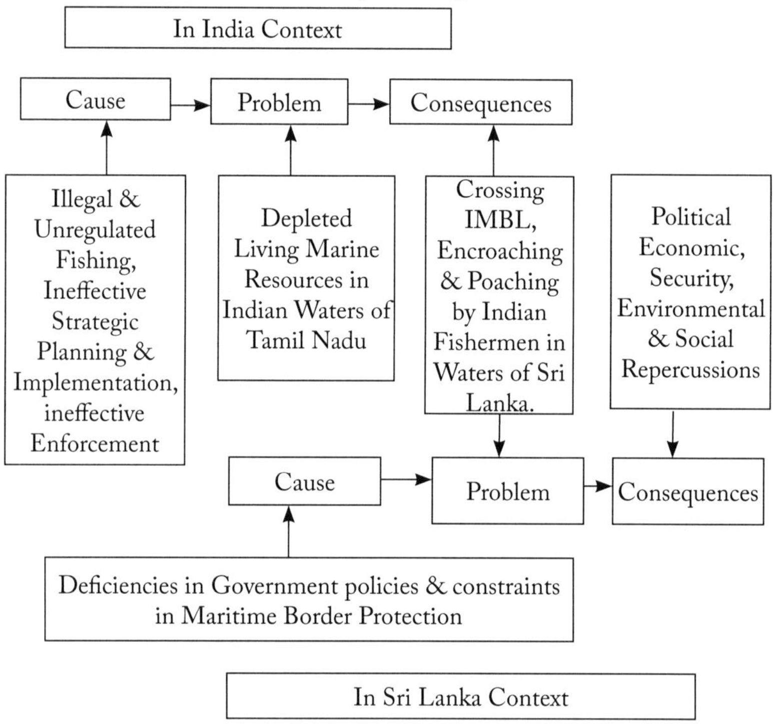

Source: Author Construction.

Perception and Approach of Indian Government

India's approach implies that it tries to promote the concept of a shared-fishing ground in Sri Lankan waters of Palk Bay and Palk Strait for fishermen of both countries, and encourages the fishing associations to move forward on that line and to formulate guidelines in sharing the Sri Lankan waters for fishing, without considering Sri Lanka's sovereignty.

India is adopting a contradictory stand with respect to the apprehensions and legal process of the poaching fishermen by arresting

Sri Lankan fishermen for poaching in Indian EEZ whilst forcing Sri Lanka to release Indian fishermen apprehended for poaching in territorial waters of Sri Lanka.

Indian government does not give due prominence to the core issue—the prevention of encroachment and poaching by Indian fishermen in Sri Lankan waters and drags its feet on the issue. Hence, a genuine effort by Indian government to prevent encroachment by Indian trawlers is very doubtful in the existing scenario due to following reasons:

- The overall relationship between Sri Lanka and India is in a stained state at present and it will influence the decisions on fisheries issues as well.
- The prevention of encroachment would not be beneficial to India.
- The prevention of encroachment would affect the livelihood of the fishing community in Tamil Nadu and create a socio-economic problem.
- Encroachment of Indian trawlers is not a threat to Indian security.
- The coalition government of India has to heed to the stand taken by Tamil Nadu government for its survival.

Perception and Approach of the State Government of Tamil Nadu

When following conclusions are considered, it is clear that Tamil Nadu government would not take genuine efforts to address the core issue of encroachment by Indian trawlers:

- During the alleged harassment by SLN, the politicians in Tamil Nadu jumped to bias and irrational conclusions within hours of the alleged incident without investigations. Hence, blaming SLN and making a political issue out of the alleged incidents is irrational and unjustified.
- Though the Indian Coast Guard confirms the encroachments, Tamil Nadu government never admits the encroaching by Indian trawlers and does not attempt to address the core issue of encroachment by Indian fishermen.
- Tamil Nadu state government is adamant on the stand that their fishermen have traditional rights for fishing in Sri Lankan waters of the Palk Bay and Palk Strait, though the claims have no legal validity.

Problem and Causes in Indian Perspective

The analyses of all relevant facts reveal that the problem in Indian context is the depletion of living marine resources in Indian waters of Tamil Nadu, as illustrated in Figure 3.9. The causes which are instrumental in creating the problem are the illegal and unregulated fishing, deficiencies in strategic planning and implementation and ineffective enforcement, which have been already discussed in the previous sub-paragraphs.

Repercussion of the Problem in Indian Perspective

The consequences of the depletion of living marine resources in Indian waters of Tamil Nadu can be broadly identified as follows:

- Indian fishing-fleet would look for living marine resources-rich areas in adjoining territories of other states in India and engage in illegal fishing;
- the catch-based incentives and wages system, and depletion of fish stocks in Indian waters would compel Indian fishermen to continue their poaching in waters of Sri Lanka, disregarding the risk of apprehension;
- the encroachment by Indian fishermen into Sri Lankan waters would lead to confrontation with Sri Lankan fishermen engaged in fishing in Sri Lankan waters;
- The law enforcement action on the encroaching Indian fishermen by Sri Lankan maritime border protection authorities would lead to political and diplomatic ramification between the two countries.

Sri Lankan Perspective

This paragraph explains the Sri Lankan perspective of the maritime border protection in Palk Bay and Palk Strait. The analyses of the facts discussed in the previous chapters clearly establish that, though the causes for the encroachment by Indian fishermen are mainly attributed to the deficiencies in the Indian policies, strategies and approach, it is Sri Lanka which has to face the ramifications. Hence, Sri Lanka has to play a major role in maritime border protection in the Palk Bay and Palk Strait. This paragraph commences with the Sri Lankan policies, strategies and approach on border protection, followed by the problem and the causes for the problem in Sri Lankan perspective, and ends with the consequences of the problem and options available for Sri Lanka to enhance its maritime border protection.

Problem and Causes in Sri Lankan Perspective

The analyses of all relevant facts reveal that the problem in Sri Lankan context is the encroaching and poaching by Indian fishermen in the waters of Sri Lanka, as illustrated in Figure 3.9. There are two major causes which are instrumental in creating the problem; one is the depletion of living marine resources in Indian waters of Tamil Nadu, which is beyond Sri Lanka's control, and the other is the deficiencies in policies and strategies related to maritime border protection adopted by Sri Lanka, which are within Sri Lanka's control. Since the causes for the depletion of living marine resources in Indian waters of Tamil Nadu have been addressed in the previous paragraph, this section focuses on the deficiencies in government policies and constraints in maritime border protection in the Sri Lankan perspective.

Deficiencies in Policies of Government of Sri Lanka

The analyses show that the following deficiencies exist in the government policies towards maritime border protection:

The soft and inconsistent law enforcement policy adopted by government of Sri Lanka towards the poaching Indian fishermen has placed constraints on the legitimate law enforcement actions in maritime border protection, making law enforcement difficult and ineffective.

When the SLN arrests encroaching Indian fishermen, Sri Lankan authorities succumb to Indian pressure and the arrested fishermen are released without initiating any legal action. The legal actions and the consequences create a deterrent effect for encroachment by Indian fishermen and the Sri Lankan government's reluctance to enforce legal process diminishes this deterrent effect.

Constraints in Maritime Border Protection

- When Sri Lankan waters are congested with hundreds of scattered Indian trawlers, it is practically impossible for a few crafts of SLN and Coast Guard to prevent poaching.
- The absence of physical barriers along the IMBL has deprived Sri Lanka of the most effective method of preventing encroachment.

- When the SLN sea patrols chase the encroaching Indian trawlers in Sri Lankan waters, SLN patrols are in a disadvantageous position as Indian trawlers can quickly reach the IMBL and enter Indian waters. Since SLN patrols cannot cross the IMBL and enter Indian waters, SLN sea patrols are unable to exercise the legitimate action of hot pursuit granted by the international law (Law of the Sea) though Indian trawlers violate the laws in Sri Lanka's territorial waters.
- The 'fear perception' of Indian fishermen towards SLN, which prevailed during the decades of war, was a deterrent for the poaching by Indian fishermen. The absence of 'fear perception' has resulted in Indian trawlers poaching well within Sri Lankan waters disregarding the presence of SLN sea patrols, until they are physically stopped by SLN. This situation has placed SLN at a disadvantages position in border protection.
- The absence of physical marking system along the IMBL, which is visible during day and night, has provided an opportunity to Indian fishermen to come up with the lame excuse of their inability to identify the IMBL.

Consequences of Existing Policies and Status of Maritime Border Protection

Sri Lanka has to face many consequences due to poaching by Indian fishermen. The consequences faced by Sri Lanka in political, economic, marine environmental, social and safety contexts have already been listed above. Hence, this paragraph confines to the consequences in border protection context.

Due to the reasons explained under Indian context, the Indian fishermen will continue their poaching in the waters of Sri Lanka, disregarding the risk of apprehension, until they are physically stopped and redirected.

The absence of fear perception for the SLN and practice of encroachment by Indian trawlers into waters of Sri Lanka disregarding the presence of SLN sea patrols in close proximity of trawlers is a dangerous scenario which might develop into uncontrollable proportions.

Sri Lankan government's policy of releasing apprehended Indian fishermen without a legal process has deprived the Sri Lankan government of vital data on poaching with legal validity, which Indian government possessed with respect to Sri Lankan fishermen. This policy deprives the Sri Lankan authorities with legally substantiated proof for Illegal, Unreported and Unregulated (IUU) fishing by Indian fishermen and valuable facts to present its case in international forums.

On the contrary, the legal action initiated by Indian authorities against Sri Lankan fishermen for illegal fishing in Indian EEZ, has provided the Indian authorities with legally substantiated proof for IUU and the European Union has strongly warned Sri Lanka on IUU fishing, citing Sri Lankan fishermen charged in Indian courts.

The absence of physical barriers along the IMBL has placed a huge burden on SLN sea patrols as SLN has to deploy sea patrols at regular intervals along the entire distance of IMBL extending close to 100 nautical miles.

When the overall situation is analysed, it is evident that SLN sea patrols alone are ineffective in the existing scenario and until a physical barrier is placed along the IMBL, the Indian fishermen will continue to encroach and trawl in Sri Lankan waters.

Necessity of Physical Identification System for IMBL and Vessels Monitoring Systems

Since the depth of water and nature of seabed along IMBL is suitable for anchoring, marker buoys should be installed to identify IMBL. This would facilitate the identification of IMBL during day and night.

Since Indian fishermen encroach into waters of Sri Lanka intentionally, introduction of better surveillance technologies such as GPS with IMBL-marked electronic charts and vessels monitoring system (VMS) would not prevent the crossing of IMBL by Indian trawlers.

Best Option for Prevention of Encroachment by Indian Trawlers

In the absence of a genuine effort by India to prevent the encroachment of Indian fishermen and the complex scenario prevailing in border protection, the best option available in Sri Lankan context is to place physical barriers by installing OFBs in Sri Lankan waters along the IMBL, at least in the most critical areas of Palk Bay and Palk Strait. The construction and installation of OFBs extending to many nautical miles is a mammoth project, but if it is done, it would be a lasting solution and the following favourable factors strengthen the option of placing OFB along IMBL.

- It would prevent all forms of unauthorised transboundary movements across the IMBL, and with each section of the barrier installed, the effectiveness of border protection would be ensured.
- It would reduce the deployment of SLN sea patrols along IMBL, thus preserving the valuable SLN resources.
- It would lead to saving of substantial financial resources, including foreign exchange, as expenses on operational and maintenance costs of SLN fleet units would be reduced.
- There would be substantial economic and social benefits, as Sri Lankan fishermen would harvest the living marine resources and would likely make a significant contribution to the economy by generating a revenue in the range of Rs. 8.6 billion annually.
- It would prevent the destruction of marine environment in Sri Lankan waters.
- The depth and nature of the sea bottom along the IMBL is suitable for anchoring the OFB segments.
- OFBs have been used in border defence in varying terrains such as outer harbours, anchorages and oil rigs in mid-sea, and so forth, and the quality assurance tests have proved the suitability of OFBs.

Recommendations

The conclusions of the study have revealed that the encroachment by Indian fishermen can be explained in two contexts; Indian and Sri Lankan contexts, as indicated Figure 3.9. This implies that the strategies to address the issue need to be formulated separately for the two contexts. The strategies needed in the Indian context and making recommendations require in-depth study of the Indian environment and systems and it is beyond the scope of this article. Hence, the strategies needed in Sri Lankan context are explained in this paragraph. The recommendations consist of approach to be followed in bilateral discussions with India, physical identification of IMBL at sea and installing OFBs along IMBL.

Sri Lanka's Approach in Bilateral Discussions

India's approach towards Sri Lanka in bilateral issues depends on India's overall relationship with Sri Lanka. Hence in the existing scenario, Sri Lanka's overall foreign policy should facilitate a win-win situation for both countries, as India would not tolerate a foreign policy perceived as hostile to India. On the issue of poaching by Indian fishermen, Sri Lanka's approach should be to counter the strategies of Indian fishermen, Tamil Nadu politicians, and the approach of the Indian government.

It is important that the stand taken by Sri Lanka is not prejudiced to the sovereignty, jurisdiction and economic interests as well as the survival of the fishing community in Sri Lanka. Similarly, if Sri Lanka agrees to any proposal which alters the status of the bilateral agreements of 1974 and 1976, it would be a disadvantage to Sri Lanka and would create many complicated issues in the future.

Sri Lanka should be very cautious about any proposal by India on designating common fishing grounds in Sri Lankan waters of the Palk Bay and Palk Strait and allowing Indian fishermen to trawl in Sri Lankan waters. The suggested guidelines in these proposals are very dangerous in the Sri Lankan context and impracticable to implement, monitor and control. If agreed, the large Indian fishing-fleet would invade Sri Lankan fishing grounds and that may lead to many serious complications in the future, paving the way for more interference by India.

Sri Lanka should insist on its right to apprehend the poaching Indian trawlers and taking legal action against them, (similar to Indian authorities), as each recorded law enforcement action would be very beneficial to Sri Lanka in future consultations between the two countries as well as in international forums.

Sri Lanka should emphasize the formulation of a common modality to expeditiously conclude the legal process with respect to apprehended fishermen in both countries, and release the fishermen after complying with court rulings.

Sri Lanka should emphasize that India implements a time-based action plan to convert trawlers in Tamil Nadu to longliner deep sea-fishing vessels and reduce the overcapacity in trawler-fleet.

Physical Identification of IMBL at Sea

Since Sri Lanka has the capability to lay marker buoys, (such marker buoys are already in operation in out-harbour), action should be initiated to lay marker buoys with day-night identification facilities, along identified locations along the IMBL. This would facilitate the identification of IMBL in day and night without any difficulty.

Recommended Long-term Solution: OFB

In the existing scenario, it is clear that the best option available in the Sri Lankan context is to place a physical barrier by installing OFBs in Sri Lankan waters along the IMBL, at least in most critical areas of the Palk Bay and Palk Strait. The construction and installation of OFBs could be carried out in stages, commencing from a pilot project with a 'sample barrier' as indicated below.

Designing and Construction of 'Offshore Sample Segment'

Since the depth and seabed is suitable for anchoring of OFBs in segments, a 'sample OFB segment' could be manufactured and tested as a pilot project.

Designing of the OFB: 'Sample Segment'

Though floating booms are being used in harbours to protect the SLN fleet, the concept of constructing and installing impact-resistant OFBs out at sea, is a new concept in the Sri Lankan context. Hence, an organisation with proficiency and experience in designing OFBs should be selected as the consultant and they should be entrusted to conduct a joint feasibility study along the IMBL with Sri Lankan authorities, and recommend the most suitable type of OFB for the intended purpose. The designed barrier should be:

- able to withstand adverse weather and sea conditions, without getting dragged from the anchored position;
- able to withstand the multiple impact of intentional crashing by Indian trawlers;
- either maintenance-free or involve minimum routine maintenance, as barriers are exposed to salty and corrosive environment.

Construction of OFB 'Sample Segment'

The first stage of the construction involves constructing a 'sample segment' of 0.5–1.0 nautical mile in length as a pilot project for testing purposes. Once the design of the OFB is finalised, there are two possible options available for construction of the 'sample segment' as indicated below.

- The first option is to explore the feasibility of constructing the 'sample segment' locally by a Sri Lankan organisation, under the supervision of an expert consultant.
- The second option is to select a suitable foreign manufacturing organisation capable of constructing the designed barrier, and construct the 'sample segment' by a foreign manufacturing company in Sri Lanka, under the combined supervision of the consultant and Sri Lanka authority.

Testing of 'Offshore Sample Barrier'

Since it is the first occasion that a 'sample segment' OFB is going to be used at the IMBL, the 'sample OFB segment' should be tested for resistance against impact and sustainability in adverse weather states.

Resistance against Impact: 'Crash Test'

The 'sample segment' should be tested for its ability to withstand multiple impacts caused by Indian trawlers and this test is known as 'Crash Test', and involves a boat moving at maximum speed and crashing against the barrier. The test should be repeated at the same point of the barrier to ascertain its ability to withstand multiple crashes. On completion of the tests, the barrier should:

- not have any major damages;
- not get dragged from its anchored location;
- return to its original position after getting dragged forward during the crash;
- not topple with the crash.

Sustainability under Adverse Operational Environment

The success of the OFB depends on its ability to remain in its original anchored position without dragging and toppling, in most adverse weather conditions. Hence, the 'sample segment' should be installed in a location close to the IMBL which is exposed to adverse weather and sea conditions during monsoons, and should be monitored continuously for its sustainability as well as for quality of materials, linking mechanisms and solar powered lights fixed on to the barrier, and so forth.

Construction and Installation of Proved OFB

Once the 'sample segment' is tested, improved and accepted, action should be initiated to construct and install the main OFB in Sri Lankan waters along the IMBL. The OFB could be installed in three stages covering the most vulnerable segment first, as indicated below.

Stage I: The first stage should cover the segments 4 indicated in Table 3.1, which extends from the north-west of Delft Island to south-west of Katchatheevu. This is the most vulnerable section of the IMBL, and involves a distance of 20 nautical miles.

Stage II: The second stage should cover the segment 5 indicated in Table 3.1, which extends from Adam's Bridge in Talaimannar to the south-west of Katchatheevu. This is the second most vulnerable section of the IMBL, and involves a distance of 15 nautical miles.

Stage III: The third stage should cover the segments 3 indicated in Table 3.1, which extends from the north-west of Karaitivu to the north-west of Delft Island. This is the third most vulnerable section of the IMBL, and involves a distance of 20 nautical miles.

Limitations and Suggestions for Future Research

The intention of the article was to address the issue of maritime border protection along the IMBL while emphasizing on intrusion by Indian fishermen, and the best possible efforts were made to obtain all possible significant data from relevant authorities and cover all factors relevant to the issue. Since there were limitations in obtaining certain data relevant to the Indian context, the article focuses more on the Sri Lankan context. Hence, it is appropriate to conduct more research on the issue, especially the Indian context as the root causes for the issue and remedial measures remain with the Indian authorities to a large extent.

Bibliography

A. G. Geobrugg, (n.d.) "Maritime Security Barriers," 2.102.04.EN.1101/1000, Romanshorn, Switzerland, www.geobrugg.com, accessed on February 25, 2011.

Asian Tribune 2012, *4th meeting of the India-Sri Lanka Joint Working Group on Fisheries.* http://www.asiantribune.com/news/2012/01/14/4th-meeting-india-sri-lanka-joint-working-group-fisheries, accessed on June 22, 2012.

"Indian premier tells SL: do not use force on Indian fishermen," *Daily mirror 2011,* (November 13, 2011). http://www.dailymirror.lk/news/14723-indian-premier-tells-sl-do-not-use-force-on-indian-fishermen.html, accessed on November 14, 2011.

"Palk Bay Fishermen's Plight and the Need of the Hour," May 2012, http://ameilie87.blogspot.com/2011/02/palk-bay-fishermens-plight-and-need-of.html, accessed on May 29, 2012.

"SL can see transformation in 15 yrs with trilingual policy: Abdul Kalam," *Dailly mirror* 2012, (January 24, 2012). http://www.dailymirror.lk/news/16292-sl-can-see-transformation-in-15-yrs-with-trilingual-policy-abdul-kalam.html, accessed on January 28, 2012.

Admiralty Chart & Publications 1584: Trincomalee to Point Calimere, 2010.

Agreement between Sri Lanka and India on the boundary in historic waters between the two countries and related matters1974, Colombo.

Agreement between Sri Lanka and India on the boundary in historic waters between the two countries 1976, Colombo.

Austin Fernando, "Tamil Nadu claim of Kachchativu ownership is not valid," *Transcurrents,* (February 18, 2012). http://transcurrents.com/news-views/archives/8261, accessed on May 29, 2012.

Divya Varkey, Ganpathiraju Pramod, Tony Pitcher, "An Estimation of Compliance of the Fisheries of India with Article 7 (Fisheries Management) of the UN code of Conduct for Responsible Fishing, in *Fisheries Centre Research Reports* University of British Columbia, Canada, vol. 14, no. 2, accessed on June 10, 2012, pp. 1–24.

Extraordinary Gazette 1996, Fishing Operation Regulations, No. 948/25, November 7, 1996.

Government of Tamil Nadu 2011, Memorandum presented to Prime Minister of India by Chief Minister of Tamil Nadu, DIPR, Secretariat, Chennai-9.

Government of Tamil Nadu 2012, Fisheries Policy Note 2012-2013, demand no.7, Thiru K A Jayapal Minister of Fisheries, Government Tamil Nadu.

Hettiarachchi A, 2007, "Fisheries in the Palk Bay Region: The Indian Factor," http://www.thehindu.com/news/cities/Madurai/state-must-also-act-to-protect-fishermen-coast-guard/article2633760.ece, accessed on November 18, 2011.

Jasper Scholtens, Maarten Bavinck, A. S. Soosai, "Fishing in Dire Straits Trans-Boundary Incursions in the Palk Bay," *Economic and Political Weekly*, vol. 47, no. 25.

K. Suresh Kumar and K. Sharath Kumar, "Design of Low Cost Maritime Boundary Identification Device using GPS System," *International Journal of Engineering Science and Technology* vol. 2, no. 9, pp. 4665–4672.

Pramod Ganapathiraju, *Illegal, Unreported and Unregulated Marine Fish Catches in the Indian Exclusive Economic Zone—Field Report* (Vancouver: MRAG, 2010).

Pramod, Ganapathiraju, "Illegal and unreported fishing: global analyses of incentives and a case study estimating illegal and unreported catches from India," (PhD diss., University of British Columbia, 2012).

Proceedings of India-Sri Lanka the joint working group on fisheries, "Fishing within the Boundaries in Northern Waters of Sri Lanka," Department of Fishery and Aquatic Resources (DFAR), Colombo, 2012.

Proclamation by His Excellency the President of Sri Lanka 1977, Colombo.

Seshadri Vasan, "Sri Lanka—India: coordinated patrol or joint patrol?" *South Asian Analysis*, paper no. 2167, http://www.southasiaanalysis.org/papers22/paper2167.html, accessed on October 15, 2011.

Sri Lanka Government 1976, *Maritime Zones Law No. 22*, Colombo.

Sri Lanka Government 1996, *Fisheries & Aquatic Resources Act No 02*, Colombo.

Sudha Ramachandran, "India fishing for trouble in Sri Lanka," Asia Times Online, (February 23, 2011), http://www.atimes.com/atimes/South_Asia/MB23Df04.html, accessed on November 18, 2011.

The Hindu, "State must also act to protect fishermen: Coast Guard," (November 17, 2011), *The National Aquatic Resources Research & Development Agency*, no. 38.

United Nations Convention on the Law of the Sea (UNCLOS), 1982.

Utopia, "Palk Bay fishermen's plight and the need of the hour," (February 24, 2011). http://ameilie87.blogspot.com/2011/02/palk-bay-fishermens-plight-and-need-of.html, accessed on June 22, 2012.

V Suriyanarayam, *Kachchativu and the Problem of Indian Fishermen in Palk Bay Region* (Chennai: TR Publication, 1994).

V Vivekanandan, "India-Sri Lanka Trans-border Fishing 2010," South Indian Federation of Fishermen Societies (SIFFS).

V Vivekanandan, "Trawl Brawl," *India—Sri Lanka Transborder Fishing*, Samudra Report no. 57, November, 2010.

V-Navy, *Barriers at Sea*, Levallois-Perret, France, www.v-navy.com, accessed on February 25, 2011.

Wijepala Tudor Jayasinghe, *Kachchativu and the Maritime Boundary of Sri Lanka* (Pannipitiya: Stamford Lake Publication, 2003).

4. Fisheries, Livelihood and Security Issues in Palk Bay

R. S. Vasan[1]

The travails of fishermen

Source: unknown

1. Commodore Vasan is currently Head of Strategy and Security Studies at the Center for Asia Studies. An alumnus of the Defence Services Staff College, College of Naval Warfare (CNW) and the International Visitor Leadership Programme, who has served the Navy and the Coast Guard with distinction. His appointments include command of warships, two naval air stations and a long-range maritime air squadron. His shore appointments include Chief Staff Officer Operations, Regional Commander of the Eastern Region of the Coast Guard, Instructor at the CNW, A Director of Naval Aviation Staff.

   Since retirement, he has served in two different think tanks and has been regularly participating in international and national seminars. He writes regularly for websites, journals and newspapers. He recently spoke at the Chatham house and also interacted with the All Parliamentary Group on Transatlantic and International Security at the British Parliament in October 2012. He has presented papers at high level international and national conferences at think tanks and professional bodies at Singapore, Melbourne, Seoul, Kunming, Johannesburg, Colombo and many national seminars in India.

   His additional assignments include, Asian Director of the World Border Organisation, Member Advisory Group at the Madras University and Stella Maris College, Executive member of the Chennai Centre for China Studies and President of the Navy Foundation, Chennai Chapter. He is also a visiting faculty at the Indian Maritime University, Academy of Maritime Education and Training and the Great Lake Institute of Management.

The issues of fisheries, livelihood and security in the Palk Bay are as old as the Palk bay itself. The fishermen from both the countries have staked claim to the rich fishing grounds in the Palk bay area. The fishing grounds in Palk Bay have witnessed the rise and fall of the Liberation Tigers of Tamil Eelam (LTTE) which ruled the seas till its defeat at the hands of the Sri Lankan military in May 2009. The study of the subject brings out some very interesting factors related to the perceptions and realities in what is now a contested area. It is difficult not to come across a print or a visual media report that does not carry news almost on a daily basis, about the frequent intrusions by Indian fishermen into Sri Lankan waters quoting their historical rights to fish in and around Katchatheevu.

The Indian fishermen exercised their fishing rights right till 1974 under the Zamindari rights of rulers of Ramnad, when India ceded Katchatheevu to Sri Lanka to demarcate the International Maritime Boundary Line (IMBL).[2] Unfortunately, it has been recorded that then Prime Minister Indira Gandhi[3] had said that it is a barren Island of little significance, little realizing that the barren Island was surrounded by rich fishing grounds of great commercial interest to fishermen from both the countries. This statement echoed similar sentiments expressed by her father who referred to Aksai chin, an area taken over by China as an area where not a blade of grass grows.[4] Both Nehru and his daughter Indira failed to understand the strategic importance of these two territories albeit at different levels both for security and livelihood issues.

Katchatheevu[5] also has another religious significance as the fishermen considered the shrine of St. Antony to be the saviour of their livelihood. It is only after the defeat of the LTTE that the annual feast of St. Antony was conducted in 2011. The feast was attended by both Indian and Sri Lankan fishermen and devotees. Indian Coast Guard (CG) and the Sri Lanka Navy coordinated the event. A total of 3387 Indian fishermen and

2. Charu Gupta and Mukul Sharma, *Contested Coastlines: Fisherfolk, Nations, and Borders in South Asia* (New Delhi: Routledge Publishers, 2008), p. 151.
3. V. Suryanarayan, *Conflict over Fisheries in the Palk Bay region* (New Delhi: Lancer Publishers & Distributors, Center for Security Analysis, 2005), p. 64.
4. Claude Arpi, *India and Her Neighbourhood: A French Observer's Views* (New Delhi: Har Anand Publications, 2005), pp. 110–111.

devotees left Rameshwaram in 114 boats on February 27. Local devotees numbering 824 also participated in the feast. It is thus expected that the old practice of holding the annual festival on the Island with participation by both the sides would be now restored. This would also ensure that the Navy and the CG would be engaged on both sides in ensuring that there are no untoward incidents and safety of the pilgrims is ensured during the passage to the Island.

In 1976, the then External Minister Swaran Singh,[6] clarified in the parliament that Indian fishermen did not have the right to crossover to the Sri Lankan side of the IMBL for fishing and, therefore, the question of either fishing or drying nets in Katchatheevu did not arise. Though the Indo-Sri Lankan IMBL has been resolved, India is yet to resolve its maritime boundary issues with the other two neighbours, Pakistan and Bangladesh.

Both in 1974 and 1976, the Tamil Nadu Government did precious little to protest if it felt that the action by the centre was not in order. It is now being argued by the State, that the Centre had no right to cede any Indian territory without a parliamentary debate and approval. The Tamil Nadu Government adopted a resolution demanding that the Island be reclaimed as the ceding of the island was unconstitutional. Former Chief Minister of Tamil Nadu Karunanidhi, the arch rival of Jayalalithaa, who did nothing all these years suddenly realised that there is merit in taking up the case with the Supreme Court and has filed a separate petition. So what was a non-issue has suddenly become an issue of great interest in the Tamil Nadu State. There are unanswered questions about why there is such unprecedented delay and inaction by the State which feels that the nearly three decade old decision was not right.

The fishermen from Tamil Nadu have never heeded to advice from any quarter and have continued to fish in troubled waters inviting the wrath of the neighbouring fishermen who are also Tamils from Sri Lanka. The Tamil Nadu fishermen had free access to the rich fishing grounds as the Sri Lankan Government had banned fishing in the areas of conflict till the defeat of the LTTE. Many fishermen used this opportunity to also

6. Suryanarayan, note 3, p. 89.

support the LTTE by smuggling essentials required for the war effort. With the defeat of the LTTE, the Sri Lankan fishermen have started fishing in their own waters and feel threatened by the intrusion of the Indian fishermen. The Sri Lankan fishermen have also objected to the use of mechanised trawlers by Indian fishermen who have indiscriminately fished in Palk bay by bottom trawling and have contributed to near complete depletion of the fish stock in Indian waters by overexploitation. The Sri Lankan fishermen rightfully fear that their fishing grounds will meet similar fate.

The routine crossing over of fishermen from India, Pakistan, Bangladesh and Sri Lanka into each other's territory is not uncommon and there are mechanisms to ensure that the fishermen are not unduly harassed due to navigational mistakes or even intentional crossing of the IMBL. A hotline was established[7] between the Indian CG and the Maritime Security Agency of Pakistan to handle crossing of fishermen into each other's territory. Pakistan has secured the release of fourteen fishermen[8] from India after taking legal recourse. Likewise, over 337 Indian fishermen, who were in Pakistani jails, have been released recently. It has been reported that these fishermen who had crossed over to Pakistan were kept in custody for many years serving prison sentences.[9] India has even set up a hotline between Islamabad and New Delhi to exchange such information. All the nations involved continue to detain erring fishermen and treat the offences as civil offences committed either intentionally or out of ignorance.[10] If India and Pakistan have a right to arrest the poaching fishermen, Sri Lanka obviously has similar responsibilities and rights in the Sri Lankan waters on their side of the IMBL. It is of course expected that due care would be taken to handle the offenders humanely.

7. Ashutosh Mishra, *India- Pakistan: Coming to Terms* (New York: Palgrave Macmillan, 2010), p. 49.
8. As reported by Tribune vide http://tribune.com.pk/story/599207/govt-paid-rs16-mln-in-fines-to-release-271-pakistanis-imprisoned-abroad/
9. Reported by Dawn http://dawn.com/news/1037801/337-indian-fishermen-released-from-pakistani-jail
10. V. Suryanarayan, *Conflict over Fisheries in the Palk Bay region* (New Delhi: Lancer Publishers & Distributors, Center for Security Analysis, 2005), p. 120.

The fishermen issue has turned political and every regional party wants to curry favour with the fishermen lobby by supporting their claims without the benefit of any impartial inquiry. To date, there is no record of any joint investigation conducted by the two nations to investigate the alleged offences committed by the Sri Lankan navy. Therefore in effect, the unproved allegations of the Tamil Nadu fishermen become the tools for political missiles to be hurled at the centre. The belligerent stand of Tamil Nadu that the Indian fishermen should have unfettered access to the sovereign fishing grounds of any neighbouring country just because there is no fish on the Indian side defies logic. It is the responsibility of the State to ensure that the fishermen are facilitated in pursuing an alternate vocation by training and rehabilitation processes if the means of livelihood are affected due to natural or man-made causes.

Some Initiatives in the Last Couple of Years

While many meetings have taken place, both at the official and unofficial levels, the visit of the former Foreign Secretary Ranjan Mathai to the island on October 11, 2011,[11] did not bring about any new solutions to the vexed issues of fishing in the troubled waters of Palk bay. All that happened was that new office-bearers revisited an age-old issue that remains unresolved and continued to struggle to find long-lasting solutions. The visit of the Foreign Secretary came in the wake of continued accusation about harassment of Indian Tamil fishermen by the Sri Lankan Navy. The Chief Minister had also written a strongly worded letter to the Prime Minister in which she said, "I would also like to emphasize that the harassment of the fishermen of Tamil Nadu should be viewed as an act of provocation and aggression against India by Sri Lanka, similar to acts of firing across the borders of India by neighbours, such as Pakistan and China." She added, "The attack on the fishermen belonging to Tamil Nadu should be viewed as a national issue and not as an isolated problem of Tamil Nadu alone."

Ranjan Mathai, who wanted to understand the issue and discuss the issue with Colombo during his visit, was briefed by the Chief Minister of

11. The visit details were reported as extracted vide http://www.asiantribune.com/news/2011/10/06/indian-foreign-secretary-ranjan-mathai-visit-sri-lanka

Tamil Nadu when he called on her en route to Colombo. His visit to the island concluded on October 11, 2011. Tamil Nadu Government has been insisting that the centre should intervene and put an end to the miseries of the fishermen by proactive measures vis-à-vis Sri Lanka. Close on the heels of the visit of the Foreign Secretary to the island, the Madurai High Court issued orders for the Central Government on October 14, 2011 to deploy the Navy/CG assets for protection of the fishermen. The court in its orders while acting on a 7-month-old public interest litigation (PIL) said, "This court is inclined to grant interim directions to the Union of India to protect the interest of the Indian fishermen against the alleged atrocities by the Sri Lankan Navy. It is needless to state that unless the Indian fishermen, particularly, Tamil fishermen are able to exercise their right to fishing, it is inherently impossible for them to survive, as they are solely depending only on the avocation of fishing and therefore, any threat to their life and security in exercising their right of fishing would ultimately infringe their fundamental right to livelihood enshrined in the constitution of India." The only point is that the fishermen who are engaged in legitimate fishing activities in their own waters need to be looked after by the designated Indian maritime agencies. However, it would indeed be a challenge to protect fishermen who have transgressed the IMBL and are poaching in Sri Lankan waters.

Joint Initiatives for Deep-Sea Fishing

Though not a new idea, the proposal for the fishermen on both sides of the IMBL to take up deep sea fishing projects on the face of it is a good one. The Sri Lankan fisheries minister at the time, Rajitha Senaratne, while expressing his disagreement suggested that India can go alone and help its fishermen to avoid troubled waters which in any case belong to Sri Lanka. He has been quoted as, "The call to go for deep-sea fishing is very good, but it should apply only to Indian fishermen," "Fishermen from North-west Lanka are fishing only in Lankan waters. It is the Indian fishermen who are intruding into Lankan waters. Therefore, it is the Indian fishermen who should move away from here and fish elsewhere." While the Sri Lankan Minister is quite correct in his assessment, the response from him clearly illustrates that there is a lot of ground to be covered before any such proposals can be received favourably without reservations to promote the cause of fishermen on both sides.

The fishermen who are fighting over the living resources are mostly Tamil fishermen from Sri Lanka and Tamil Nadu. Sri Lanka Minister expressed a view that while Sri Lanka engaged in responsible fishing on its side (by not using mechanised trawlers) has no need to share its wealth with aggressive Tamil Nadu fishermen who have not respected the maritime boundaries. By using mechanised trawlers, the greedy owners have been compelling the daily wage earning fishermen to resort to unfair practices and indulging in fishing in Sri Lankan waters. Indian fishermen are not only fishing around the disputed Katchatheevu Islands quoting historical rights but also venturing close to the Sri Lankan coasts, thus inviting the wrath of the Sri Lankan fishermen and the Navy. It may be recalled that on February 21, 2011, over 400 Sri Lankan Tamil fishermen protested in front of the Indian Consulate Office in Jaffna about intrusion by Indian fishermen.

Tamil Nadu Government Stand

Coming to the much debated issue of fishing, the Chief Minister of Tamil Nadu routinely accuses the Sri Lankan navy of harassing the Indian fishermen and sends out letters to the Prime Minister. The detention of the Tamil Nadu fishermen and their boats has been played up by the State Government which wants strong diplomatic action to be initiated against Sri Lanka. The undisputed fact of the matter is that Tamil Nadu fishermen regularly fish in disputed waters of Sri Lanka not just off Katchatheevu but well inside the Sri Lankan waters. The Sri Lankan Government has also started vigorous patrols on its side to prevent poaching and has detained many Indian fishermen who have strayed in to the Sri Lankan waters well beyond even the Katchatheevu Island. The fishermen from Sri Lanka, a majority of who are also Tamils, come into conflict with Tamil Nadu fishermen over depleting resources. It is common knowledge that fishermen resolutely protect their territory anywhere in the world. The Tamil Nadu fishermen who stray into the adjoining state of Andhra or Kerala are also held hostage by the fishermen association and are released only after a penalty is paid. This has led to local conflict[12] in each other's fishing grounds.

Whether right or wrong, the demarcation of the IMBL in 1974 puts Katchatheevu on the Sri Lankan side. The Indian fishermen are known to use the banned bottom trawling methods which denude the fishing grounds. Whenever they are attacked in Sri Lankan waters, the complaint is that they were attacked in Indian waters. This is done to ensure that the compensation claims, if any, are entertained by the Tamil Nadu Government. No claims would be admitted for incidents in Sri Lankan waters. In a recent report provided by the Government based on a right to information (RTI), it has been indicated that all the attacks are shown as having taken place in Indian waters in the first information reports. Regrettably, there is no record of any joint investigation or evidence to prove or disprove the alleged attacks. The Indian CG, while filing an affidavit in Madurai, categorically observed that there are no attacks/apprehending of Indian fishermen by Sri Lankan Navy in Indian waters. Even fishermen from the Indian side acknowledge in private that they do cross the IMBL regularly due to lack of living resources on the Indian side. Many fishermen are daily wage earners and are at the mercy of the owners of trawlers who force the fishermen to crossover to rich fishing grounds on the other side of the IMBL.

According to an RTI activist, there have been many cases filed by the fishermen who claimed that they were attacked by the Sri Lankan Navy. Unfortunately, these cases have not been investigated and pursued to their logical conclusion. The CG was also drawn into the controversy and was required to provide an affidavit in the Madurai high court about the facts of the case. The statement by the CG that the Indian fishermen were indeed straying into the Sri Lankan waters, though factual, was not liked by the State Government. The CG and the Indian Navy maintain that there have been no firing incidents in the Indian waters and have been categorical that the Sri Lankan navy does not enter Indian waters to apprehend the Indian fishermen. The Indian CG and the Indian Navy

12. *Times of India*, "TN, AP fishermen at war," http://articles.timesofindia.indiatimes.com/2011-08-14/chennai/29886338_1_fishermen-mechanised-boats-andhra-pradesh, August 15, 2011.

also meet their counterparts every quarter at the IMBL and discuss these issues. Invariably, such meetings reinforce the fact that the Indian fishermen continue to violate the IMBL routinely. This is also supported by radar pictures taken by both the sides. Indian fishermen have no qualms in admitting that they indeed cross the IMBL and fish in Sri Lankan waters as there is no fish on the Indian side.

Need for Joint Investigation

In the light of many incidents, where it is alleged even without any formal investigation that the Indian fishermen are being attacked by the Sri Lankan Navy even in Indian waters, there is a need to have a robust mechanism that caters to joint investigation with access to modern aids that are available and mutually agreed processes.

Joint Initiatives by Fishermen/Non-governmental Organisation (NGOs) on Either Side

There have been both unofficial and official meetings that have tried to resolve the issues of fishing in an amicable manner. However, as long as some of the core issues do not get addressed, suspicions would remain. Any concessions extended to the Tamil Nadu fishermen by the Sri Lanka Government by way of perpetual leasing or multi-day fishing would make the Sri Lankan fishermen (majority of who are Tamils) feel that their interests are being compromised by the majority Sinhala Government. The Sri Lankan Government which is already being accused of a majority bias cannot afford to alienate its own Tamil fishermen on the issue. The dialogue between the fishing communities and the NGOs on both sides must continue as it would provide a platform for the two sides to appreciate the compulsions on either side and, therefore, could enable a meeting point aided by State support on the initiatives.

In addition to exploring other avenues for facilitating the fishermen along the coastal belt of Ramnad to pursue other vocational training, the answer lies in ensuring that the Indian fishermen are trained in deep-sea fishing on modern fishing vessels in the exclusive economic zone (EEZ) which extends up to 200[13] nautical miles from the coastline. India is blessed with over two million km^2 of EEZ and there are many areas which are routinely poached by other nationals, including Sri Lankan fishing vessels. There have been a number of recommendations given by experts, academia and NGOs about finding a lasting solution to the problems of fishermen. Many options have been provided for consideration of the stakeholders. Unfortunately, there is not much headway to provide alternate means of employment and equipping the traditional fishermen with better skills and equipment for deep-sea fishing.

When it comes to Sri Lanka, it is clear that the State and the Centre's views are contradictory on most occasions. The United Progressive Alliance (UPA) Government was accused of providing military hardware along with China and other nations to defeat the LTTE, a terrorist organisation. Even Jayalalithaa did not have a second opinion about banning the LTTE and had constantly supported actions to defeat them. However, due to the international pressure and the lobbying efforts of the Tamil diaspora about the human rights violations in the final phases of the war has contributed to hardening of the stand, particularly of the Tamil community and the Tamil Nadu Government. This resulted even in objection for training of military personnel in India by the Tamil Nadu Government. The Indian Government has done well to clarify that it will continue to train the military personnel from our neighbouring countries, including Sri Lanka. The State has to realise that the training of military personnel from our neighbouring countries has a strategic connotation and has brought the military personnel of the countries closer and enables cooperation for taking on the common threats in the region by bilateral agreements. It also provides many options for future. By denying training to Sri Lanka or any other nation, India will lose out an opportunity to engage with the military establishment and maintain lateral interactions at appropriate levels in our neighbourhood. As has been demonstrated, the military personnel at different levels who are exposed to excellent training facilities and infrastructure in India would remain India's friends forever.

13. Bharat Verma, ed., *Indian Defence Review Oct-Dec 2012* (New Delhi: Lancer International, 2012), p. 12.

Joint Patrol by the Indian and Sri Lankan Maritime Forces

This is another issue that keeps surfacing every now and then without making much headway.[14] The proposal for joint patrolling by Indian and Sri Lankan navies is nothing new and has been discussed at length on many occasions, including during the meeting of the joint working group on fisheries. Sri Lanka during different phases of the Eelam war was very keen to have this format that would serve to prevent LTTE from using Tamil support for supporting its war efforts. It is public knowledge that many fishermen did engage in smuggling essential goods to LTTE for commercial consideration. The Indian Government on its part has not been able to make up its mind due to the indirect pressure from Tamil Nadu Government based on fears that this would also imply total ban on our fishermen crossing-over to the other side, including areas around Katchatheevu, which is haunted by historical claims that clash with the IMBL agreement of 1974 which ceded this island to Sri Lanka.

The Indian Navy and the Indian CG who patrol these areas are well aware that hundreds of boats crossover to the other side and indulge in fishing. Any force to prevent them from crossing would also result in backlash against the central forces and result in strained relations between the Centre and the State. The joint patrolling is indeed a good idea; however, the Government of India and the Tamil Nadu Government must clearly understand that the maritime security agencies cannot prevent the arrest of our fishermen from Sri Lankan Law enforcement authorities for entering their areas and vice versa due to a highly charged atmosphere in the Palk Bay, which has brought the fishermen into conflict with the law enforcement agencies on both sides. The procedure is followed with respect to offenders from other countries who enter the EEZs of India. However, time and again, it has been reiterated that such offenders anywhere in the world are tried under civil offences act and are not to be ill-treated or shot at as alleged by the fishermen. This also brings out another issue of joint investigation. There is no way of establishing the veracity of the statements of fishermen unless there is an impartial joint investigation with access to

14. Also see Author's article carried by SAAG http://www.southasiaanalysis.org/papers22/paper2167.html .

all records and evidence. The pattern, thus far, has been that the Indian fishermen complain that they were shot at or their fish catch looted while in Indian waters. The fishermen privately admit that they have no choice but to cross the boundaries and fish in Sri Lankan waters as they would not be paid their wages by the owners of the boat who insist on the boats bringing back fish from any part of the ocean, including sovereign waters/ EEZ of another country.

It would be wise on part of the Indian Government to agree to the joint patrol proposal as it would clearly bring out the facts in any reported cases of harassment or firing without bias. However, the ground situation today is such that unless the Tamil Nadu Government is in a position to provide the fishermen alternate means of livelihood, including deep-sea fishing, the starving fishermen (most of them are wage earners), driven by the need to engage in their vocation at whatever cost, would not heed the advice of the Navies/CGs/Marine Police Wing to stop from crossing-over in pursuit of fishing grounds. An ill-planned, hasty implementation of the joint patrol without first addressing the core issues of low yields on the Indian side and deep-sea fishing avenues would not only incur the wrath of the fishermen but also would strain bilateral and navy-to-navy relations.

Tamil Nadu Initiatives

The Chief Minister who has shown a lot of concern about the welfare and safety of the fishermen has demonstrated her willingness to take this issue head on. During the address by Finance Minister Panneerselvam on August 4, 2011,[15] some of the problems of the fishermen have been sought to be remedied. By its own admission, vide budget speech available at the State has achieved a marine fish production of 4.04 lakh tonnes against a potential of 7 lakh tonnes (nearly 40 percent gap). Similarly, inland fish production is only 1.71 lakh tonnes against a potential of 4.5 lakh tonnes (60 percent gap). Of the 56,000 fishing vessels, only 6000 are mechanised. A total of 25 crore have been set aside to promote acquisition of deep-sea fishing vessels.[16] The

15. Government of Tamil Nadu, "Budget Speech Delivered by the Chief Minister of Tamil Nadu," Full text available at http://www.tn.gov.in/budget/Revised_Budget_Speech_e_2011_2012.pdf, accessed on August 12, 2012.
16. Ibid.

State has announced that it would provide a subsidy of up to 5 lakh for those procuring deep-sea vessels and aims to add about 500 deep-sea tuna liners to the capacity for deep-sea fishing.

While the initiative is laudable, it is clear that these projects would take considerable time before the benefits are felt by the community. The statement of Dr A. S. Soosai, an activist in the fishermen's movement and a Professor of Geography at Jaffna University has observed that, "Firstly, the deep seas are too far for them. Secondly, the fishermen here do not have multi-day boats with satellite communication equipment. To buy such a vessel they need around $91,000. They also need training and the port facilities. None of these is available now." This statement is equally applicable to Indian fishermen who would need state support and sustained initiatives to get away from the coastal waters with depleting or near extinct fish stock.

The Tamil Nadu Government has also enhanced the relief amount during the period of fisheries ban to Rs 4000 and expects to incur an additional expense of 72 crore. There is a need to fully utilise the potential of the Fisheries Department. The Tamil Nadu Fisheries Development Corporation (TNFDC) needs to expand the scope of its activities to promote the interests of fishermen. Obviously for this to happen, there is a need for revamping of the TNFDC. Working out long-term/short-term plans and ensuring availability of sufficient funds on a sustained basis is required for TNFDC to take up deep-sea fishing with the seriousness that it deserves. The period of ban from April 15 for 45 days during which the fishermen lay off work should in addition be used by the TNFDC to provide training that would equip the fishermen to take up the challenges of deep-sea fishing.

Some Options

Many studies have been conducted and many out of the box suggestions have been made to declare the Palk bay waters as waters of common heritage. However, the proposal is unlikely to find favour with the Sri Lankan counterparts as they perceive it as a measure that will only take away their share of living resources which rightly belongs to them. This has been a non-starter till now and is likely to just fade away.

There has also been a suggestion that a perpetual lease of the fishing grounds around Katchatheevu would be a good idea as there are past precedents of similar leasing arrangements with Sri Lanka. Analysts quote the precedent of allowing Sri Lankan fishermen to fish in the Wadge Bank near Cape Comorin for a period of three years from 1976.[17] However, many in Sri Lanka do not seem to remember that India was accommodative of the request for this concession provided to Sri Lanka. Unfortunately, in an era of dwindling fish stocks and increased competition for living resources, this is also unlikely to be received well by the Sri Lankan counterparts.

Another suggestion that was made was in the form of a representation made by the National Fishworkers Forum to the Prime Minister on April 08, 2013, to set up the India Sri Lanka Maritime Authority (ISMA) to resolve such disputes merits serious consideration. The forum has indicated that there are similar provisions in other parts of the world such as Japan, Korea and Russia for resolving such disputes. The ISMA would help in resolving long-standing issues in Palk Bay as long as both the nations work together and have a dynamic model that would address the issues in the Palk Bay.

Despite some of the practical difficulties that may be experienced on ground, the Centre and the State should seriously consider implementing this suggestion and should also empower the ISMA to investigate all incidents in the respective fishing areas. A lot of preparatory work is required by both India and Sri Lanka if this proposal is to be adopted and rendered workable. While it will not solve the problem of lack of fish stock in the area, at least ISMA will be equipped and empowered to mediate between the two sides that are fighting over dwindling resources on either side of the IMBL.

For the first time, the Tamil Nadu vision paper 2023 has a provision for deep-sea fishing vessels to be acquired. This needs to be expedited and more deep-sea fishing vessels and even floating factories are required to be procured along with the supporting cold chain over land that will help in export.

---

17. V. Suryanarayan, *Conflict over Fisheries in the Palk Bay region* (New Delhi: Lancer Publishers & Distributors, Center for Security Analysis, 2005), p. 97.

Conclusion

In conclusion, it is a considered opinion of the author that India and the Tamil Nadu Government have a lot more to do in comparison with its small neighbour. There is no need for looking at concessions from our southern neighbour to protect the fishermen, particularly in the context of possession of an EEZ that has blessed India with a sea area of 2.1 million km^2. There are many schemes that have been launched by the present Government in Tamil Nadu which need to be fast-paced and supported. There has to be a time-bound programme for weaning the small time fishermen from coastal fishing and provide them a better opportunity for harvesting the fish catch in our own EEZ. While the fishermen on both sides are engaged in dialogue, it can only gain meaning if there is parallel proactive action to address the shortcomings in our capacity and capability to fish in our own waters.

Bibliography

Ashutosh Mishra, *India-Pakistan: Coming to Terms* (New York: Palgrave Macmillan, 2010).

Bharat Verma, ed., *Indian Defence Review Oct-Dec 2012* (New Delhi: Lancer International, 2012).

Charu Gupta and Mukul Sharma, *Contested Coastlines: Fisherfolk, Nations, and Borders in South Asia* (New Delhi: Routledge Publishers, 2008).

Claude Arpi, *India and Her Neighbourhood: A French Observer's Views* (New Delhi: Har Anand Publications, 2005).

Government of Tamil Nadu, "Budget Speech Delivered by the Chief Minister of Tamil Nadu," http://www.tn.gov.in/budget/Revised_Budget_Speech_e_2011_2012.pdf, accessed on August 12, 2012.

V. Suryanarayan, *Conflict over Fisheries in the Palk Bay region* (New Delhi: Lancer Publishers & Distributors, Center for Security Analysis, 2005).

5. Examining the Fisheries Issues at the Maritime Boundary between India-Pakistan and India-Bangladesh

Prabhakaran Paleri[1]

Marine fisheries can cause geostrategic issues that may demand serious learning among national security planners. Among the agents of maritime issues, marine fisheries activities historically add up in breeding conflicts among nations at the least expected times. Often, the reports were prevaricated and shaded by the complainants seeking and emphasizing protectionist viewpoints for social as well as political reasons more than safeguarding the genuine interests of the fishers, on one hand, as the traditional hunter gatherers of the ocean and, on the other, the ocean ecology that is vital to life over land. The welfare of fishers can get damaged in the absence of a socially reformed and organised fishery sector. They, in turn, damage the ocean ecology focused on instant survival. They take advantage of the situation and continue their engagement with the ocean and its environment without serious concern for sustainability. Littoral nations, including the small island nations, face a host of issues in governing and managing marine fisheries. The issues include illegal, unreported and unregulated (IUU) fishing and the collaterals in the form of:

- marine environmental damage
- maritime boundary violations
- depletion of fisheries sources
- illegal transfers at sea
- unlawful activities at and from the sea in the guise of fishing

1. The author is the former director general of Indian Coast Guard and presently, visiting academician and research scholar. The views expressed are exclusively from the findings of the author and do not reflect policies of any government or formal body of decision makers.

- security challenges
- conflicts and clashes
- coastal zone degradation and so forth

For many nations, marine fisheries excite pressure points in national governance. The subject is quite complex to graphically unveil and present as a singular topic as there are many elements in fisheries issues, each demanding serious and separate study.

Population pressure is also a factor that escalates the demand for marine aquatic food sources and amplifies the problems the fishers and the nations face. Pirate fishers violate every law of fisheries, where they exist, lured by strong economic incentive. All these call for the need for nations and international organisations to engage in effective management of the consumption pressures on marine fisheries. The UN Food and Agricultural Organization (FAO) is quite concerned about the depletion of fisheries sources in the world's fishing grounds. According to the FAO, 70 percent of the world's commercially important marine fish stocks are fully fished, overexploited or depleted.[2] Scholars and experts involved in the study of marine fisheries feel that there is already a global fisheries crisis that will need serious attention to identify remedial measures. The cause for it is escalating demand, rapid technological progress and massive government subsidies. There are surplus fishing vessels that lead to extended overfishing accelerating the depletion of stock and threatening marine biodiversity. Developed and developing countries are equally affected by the impact. What alarms the FAO is the aggressive industrial fishing. Industrial fishers hunt for high-value fish and sweep them off the ocean.

The Code of Conduct for Responsible Fisheries (1995) that is also called the UN Fisheries Code or FishCode, introduced by the FAO in 1995, breaks the ancient belief that fisheries sources were an unlimited gift of nature. The code provides direction to ensure that these resources, renewable but not unlimited, are exploited in a

2. Lisa Speer, "Marine Fisheries, Population and Consumption: Science and Policy Issues," (September 1995). www.aaas. org/ international/ehn/fisheries/speer.htm.

sustainable manner the world over. The code was the fallout of this awareness, especially in the post United Nations Convention on the Law of the Sea (UNCLOS)[3] world. The code deals with marine as well as other forms of fisheries including aquaculture. The code is voluntary, though certain parts of it are based on international law. It is yet to be taken seriously by the nations of the world. There are loud complaints that most nations ignore or fail to abide by the UN Fisheries Code.[4] Studies indicate that the compliance rate scored by Australia, Norway, the United States, Canada, Iceland and Namibia was above 60 percent.[5] According to researchers, the overall conclusion about the long-term sustainability of the world fisheries sources was depressing. They prompt the United Nations to make the code mandatory. Mandatory regulations may not be acceptable to almost all the countries in the world for various socio-economic and political reasons. The situation also speaks largely about the lack of understanding among nations about the business, occupational and natural environment of fisheries in the world.

Another aspect that needs attention, especially in this study, is about the transboundary nature of marine fisheries resulting in dispute and conflict scenarios between nations. In a wider sense, it has been mentioned as poaching, which means trespassing into another's property with an intention to take game or fish. It is an unlawful activity that may extend to further unlawful activities in the guise of fishing. Nations have to be cautious about it. Poaching need not be between neighbours alone but can also involve slim customers from long distance. Though ocean poaching is a term widely used for stealing fish from another's or one's own territory by violating the laws, in its expanded form it amounts to illegal hunting or gathering and taking away or destroying ocean resources by stealth and also causing

3. United Nations Convention on the Law of the Sea, 1982, provided a new framework for the management of ocean resources.
4. John Heilprin, "Most Nations 'Ignore UN Fisheries Code," *The Sydney Morning Herald*, (February 2009). news.smh.com.au/breaking-news-world/most-nations-ignore-un-fisheries-code-20090205-7y2y.html.
5. Ibid.

collateral damages. It may go beyond fisheries. All these impinge on national security in its wholesome context.[6]

Within the ambit of poaching, fisheries management and control has become a global issue with multitudinous fallouts in the realm of unlawful activities at sea. Another interesting aspect of poaching is that while some waters become troubled by poaching, some poach in troubled waters.[7] For example, a disputed water, where the nations concerned have not come to an agreement under 'consensus ad idem', can be declared as troubled waters. Poaching in such waters has to be seen differently from poaching across borders that are well demarcated. Most of the borders that are still disputed in the world are troubled waters.

Today, regulating poaching anywhere in the world is under the age-old practice of enforcement agencies, apprehending them and seizing their boats and catch. Sometimes the enforcement agencies even resort to firing upon poachers. Fishers are also shot at under suspicion of piracy or as agents of insurgency. Many fishers escape under the barrage of gunfire. Some go home crippled, some get killed. There will be political uproars, media reports, bureaucratic meetings and finally, monetary compensations to anoint the wounds. But usually, it is time that will silence the noise before new issues begin. Policies or bilateral understandings are not taken seriously neither by the governments nor by the poachers. Everyone will look at gaining mileage under perplexity rather than bringing permanent closure to such occurrences. There were incidents when nations even came to the brink of war. The Code wars between Britain and Denmark between 1958 and 1976 were examples. It also shows the geostrategic impact of marine fisheries. Today, code or shrimp wars caused by alleged fisheries poaching are fought in diplomatic enclaves between responsible nations, not in the open sea.

The threats the marine fisheries and, by it, the nations face today can be summed up as,

6. The wholesome concept visualises national security beyond military security as identified by the author and published in his book *National Security: Imperatives and Challenges* (New Delhi: Tata McGraw-Hill Publishing Limited, 2008).
7. Prabhakaran Paleri, *Maritime Security: the Unlawful Dimension* (New Delhi: Magnum Books Pvt. Ltd, 2010), p. 164.

- depletion of species,
- habitat loss,
- pollution, and
- conflicts.

Here, the solution is not only managing marine fisheries efficiently but also conflict resolution and marine environmental as well as resource protection. This study examines how these aspects reflect at the yet-to-be demarcated Indo-Pakistan and Indo-Bangladesh maritime boundaries. It may be prudent to examine the issues and problems, if any, faced by the three countries in the field of marine fisheries before examining the 'suspended' boundaries at sea.

India and Marine Fisheries

India has a 7,517 km coastline opening out to the Indian Ocean. The country claims 12 nautical miles of territorial sea, 24 nautical miles of contiguous zone, 200 nautical miles of exclusive economic zone and a continental shelf of 200 nautical miles or to the outer edge of the continental margin.[8]

India ranks third in the world in total fish production.[9] India contributes nearly 5 percent towards the global fish production. The Indian fisheries sector is growing consistently. But within these overall findings, performance suggests that fisheries management in India meets only a few policy outcomes against the stated planning goals established by the government.[10] India needs to move towards sustainable net economic benefits if the gains from marine fisheries have to be optimised under the criteria of economic development. This is especially so, considering India's track record in fish production and the opportunities available to develop the marine fisheries sub-sector by building more productive fish stocks. India needs to adopt modern fishing knowledge, follow strict regulatory

8. Prabhakaran Paleri, *Coast Guards of the World and Emerging Maritime Threats* (Tokyo: Ocean Policy Research Foundation, 2009), p. 59. As compiled from various sources. Readers are advised to verify with government sources on the present stand of the country.
9. "The World Bank, India Marine Fisheries, 2011," www.indiaenvironmentportal.org.in/files/file/India_ Marine_ fisheries.pdf.
10. Ibid.

regime and introduce reforms and sustainability policies in the marine fisheries sub-sector. The growth in fish production has not reflected in the economic well-being of the people involved. Besides, India seemingly is yet to appreciate the problems that its marine fisheries encounter for proactive consideration of regulatory policies advocated by the FAO. India lags in many ways in sustainable and responsible fisheries management in spite of its burgeoning bureaucracy and fisheries agencies.

At the centre, the Ministry of Agriculture manages the fishing industry through various agencies and organisations under it. The federal structure of India is often quoted while discussing problems of regulatory measures of marine fisheries. There should not be hindrance of any kind to marine fisheries if the central and state governments are cohesive in managing fisheries though there are isolated calls for bringing marine fisheries in the concurrent list of the constitution. There are a number of laws, especially at the central level, relevant to the overall fisheries sectors that should be read in conjunction with one another in regulating the marine fisheries sub-sector. This could also be said about the agencies that deal in various activities related to fisheries in India. The problems with marine fisheries, in spite of various laws and agencies, are that there are no control by entry restrictions, retirement of old fishing fleets and legal action against violators. It is quite a free and liberalised zone of activity more in welfare mode than in economic form and shape. The regulatory measures in place include closure of fishing season and areas, marine protected areas and species, ban on destructive fishing gears and methods, mesh and legal size restrictions and turtle exclusive devices in trawls near notified rookeries. According to a study, the issues India faces in marine fisheries are varied.[11] They include primarily,

- declining catches,
- post-harvest losses,
- habitat degradation,
- climate change impact,

11. P. U. Zachaeria, "Present and Future Scenario of Indian Marine Fisheries," cmfri.org.in/uploads_en/divisions/files/Present%20and%20future%20scenario%20of%20Indfian%20marine%20fisheries.pdf.

- IUU fishing, and
- enforcement gap.

The interesting aspect of Indian marine fisheries is that none of the studies seriously mention any problem the fishers encounter at the maritime borders of the country and its impact on Indian fisheries. There is no reference about problems of fishers at the boundaries of India and Pakistan or Bangladesh and India. The reason could be that the issues are geopolitical and more so geostrategic than marine fisheries in the perception of the fisheries authorities.

India is yet to seriously follow the UN Fisheries Code. The compliance rate is about 36 percent which is considered much below the lower level.[12] It will augur well with India to follow the code but that could provoke sociopolitical resistance because of the diverse nature of the fishery culture in India even in marine fisheries.

Pakistan and Marine Fisheries

Pakistan has a 1,046 km coastline along the Arabian Sea. Its maritime zone claims are 12 nautical miles of territorial sea, 24 nautical miles of contiguous zone, 200 nautical miles of exclusive economic zone and a continental shelf of 200 nautical miles or to the outer edge of the continual margin.[13]

Like India, Pakistan too is seriously dependent on marine fisheries in its economic development. The coastline of Pakistan is shorter than that of India, opening to the Arabian Sea. But nevertheless, the country is rich in marine fishery sources. The fisheries sources have great potential for development. People of the coastal states of Sindh and Balochistan are engaged in marine fisheries. The Ministry of Food, Agriculture and Livestock manages the fishing industry in Pakistan. The ministry is responsible for fishery in the high seas of the exclusive

12. Ibid.
13. Prabhakaran Paleri, *Coast Guards of the World and Emerging Maritime Threats* (Tokyo: Ocean Policy Research Foundation, 2009), p. 87. As compiled from various sources. Readers are advised to verify with government sources on the present stand of the country.

economic zone, making policies, inter-provincial coordination, fisheries management, and so forth, as in the case of the federal system of governance.

Marine fisheries sub-sector of Pakistan employs a large number of people, directly and indirectly, in ancillary industries. The industry is also export oriented. The contribution is about 0.25 percent of the world exports.

The issues of Pakistan fisheries are of technical, operational and regulatory nature. They include,

- under exploitation,
- high post-harvest losses,
- fisheries harbour congestion,
- storage capacity and technical constraints,
- enforcement of fisheries discipline,
- limitations in fish processing for export, and
- coastal environmental issues.[14]

There are efforts to modernise marketing procedures, capacity enhancement, vessel improvement, coastal infrastructure development, fisheries training, and so forth. The Pakistan fisheries fall much below India in regard to compliance with the UN Fisheries Code.

Bangladesh and Marine Fisheries

Bangladesh has 580 km coastline along the Bay of Bengal. The country claims 12 nautical miles of territorial sea, 18 nautical miles of contiguous zone and 200 nautical miles of an exclusive economic zone. The claim on the continental shelf is up to the outer limits of the continental margin.[15]

14. Pakissan, "Agri overview: Fisheries sector in Pakistan," pakissan.com/english/ agri. overview/ fisheries.sector.in.pakistan.shtml, and "Brief on Environmental Problems of the Marine and Coastal Areas," www.environment.gov.pk/PRO_PDF/PositionPaper/ Marine%20pollution.pdf.
15. Prabhakaran Paleri, *Coast Guards of the World and Emerging Maritime Threats* (Tokyo: Ocean Policy Research Foundation, 2009), p. 59. As compiled from various sources. Readers are advised to verify with government sources on the present stand of the country.

The coastline of Bangladesh is slightly more than half the coastline of Pakistan. It is open to the Bay of Bengal which is a rich habitat for exploitable marine species. Bangladesh has a large fleet of artisanal and coastal fisheries. The contribution of marine fisheries is less than inland fisheries. Bangladesh is experiencing a decline in both the fisheries outputs. Though Bangladesh exports fisheries products, the marine fisheries sector needs further support through governmental policies for exploitation and export promotion. The issues that need attention of the government of Bangladesh in marine fisheries are:

- overall development of marine fisheries sector,
- technical and skill development,
- infrastructure development,
- marketing support,
- export promotion, and
- developing international and regional networks.[16]

The Ministry of Fisheries and Livestock is the central ministry for marine fisheries and other aspects according to the rules of business in Bangladesh. The country is one of the leading inland fish producers. Marine fisheries production is less than one third of inland production. It is also a matter of taste and culture and not of any geographical disadvantage alone. The country has the potential to go in for marine fishers at least from the point of view of export promotion.

Summing up the Issues of Marine Fisheries: Bangladesh, India and Pakistan

Marine fishery is a serious industry with an economic yield in all the three countries out of which India has a comparatively developed export-based organisation. However, India falls back in the sustainable exploitation of its vast marine fisheries sources and developing its export potential. It is no different for Pakistan and Bangladesh. All the three countries need to follow aggressive policies in exploiting their marine fisheries to its fullest potential

16. Humayun Kabir, "Marine Fisheries in Bangladesh: an Overview," library.enaca.org/NACA-Publications/MaricultureWorkshop/MaricultureWS2006_Bangladesh.pdf.

in a sustainable manner. The projected issues in the marine fisheries subsector are more or less common to all the three countries examined. But the interesting fact is that nowhere is there a serious reference to border clashes of fishers either between India and Pakistan or India and Bangladesh. Border issues, if any, are not seriously reflected in the fishery sector and, therefore, have to be examined with respect to the enforcement or, more acutely, with the geopolitical issues of the respective countries. It is also not clear at this stage whether such issues, if existing, are seriously impacting on the fisheries production or trade of the three countries. It does not seem to be so.

Fisheries law enforcement is carried out by various organisations in all the three countries. In a federal set-up that the three countries follow, it is generally the role of the state or provincial governments to establish the rule of law in the territorial sea. The central forces and agencies establish the law in the high seas beyond the territorial sea in the exclusive economic zones, where the countries have jurisdiction over living and nonliving resources in the water column, seabed as well as subsoil and for other economic activities as specified in Article 56 of the UNCLOS.

All the three countries—Bangladesh, India and Pakistan—have various agencies with the state, provincial and central governments to establish the law at sea. However, demarcating them for territorial waters or highs seas will become a complex issue when the disputes are about the boundaries in the territorial sea extending to the high seas. The question is, 'which force or agency will handle the issue at a particular point or location at sea—central or state?' This is another interesting factor which many countries have not seriously examined.

An aspect that the author would like to mention here at this stage, though strictly not as an inclusive part of this paper, is that under the federal law, where it is the state or provincial governments that are responsible for the rule of law in their jurisdiction, it need not be so under exception in the territorial waters as it is a concept based on UNCLOS, which is the law of the sea and not land-based or the 'law of the land', unlike other aspects of jurisdiction. Under this argument, territorial sea is 'not an extension of land' under law but a place extraneous to its land territory where a nation has absolute sovereignty. Thereby, it does not become a direct extension of the state, union territory or province but an area where the state, union territory or province has jurisdiction under sovereignty. The central forces, under this argument, can be very much there, and are there to establish and execute their charter. It is an exclusive exception for maintaining sovereignty in the ocean terrain. Of course, the governments have not tried it out except in certain cases by practice, where the coast guards patrol territorial waters for search and rescue or even the point of boundaries of adjacent maritime nations in the territorial sea, historical waters or archipelagic waters, whether disputed or otherwise. If not, no central forces can be in territorial waters or waters of similar jurisdiction like in the historical, archipelagic or similar waters. It should be the exclusive realm of the state or provincial governments. The argument here is that it is not if it is ocean based. This aspect is mentioned in this paper primarily to explain that territorial sea is not an extension of land but an extension of sovereignty. There is a difference.

By practice, the issue has been overlooked so far in maritime disputes and normally, it is central forces like the coast guard or the navy that get involved. The problem gets aggravated if the navies get involved as they are military forces meant for combat. Most of the nations prefer coast guards or similar agencies that have more acceptability than a force of combat in other-than-war situations.[17]

The Maritime Border: India–Pakistan

India and Pakistan share a long-standing maritime boundary dispute in Sir Creek and adjoining areas in the Rann of Kutch over about 96 km strip of water dividing both the countries. The Sir Creek dispute is documented to have originated in 1875 between the two princely states of Sindh and Kutch of the British colonial India. Sindh is now in Pakistan and Kutch is a district in Gujarat, India. The Government of Bombay, under the British, took up the case in 1907–1908 and after consultations with both the sides, brokered an agreement and promulgated its decision in a letter dated September 20,

17. Other-than-war situation is the situation when there is no war. This is a term coined by the author in his research studies as the idea of 'peace' is an abstract term and considered inappropriate in strategic use. The world goes through two situations: war and other-than-war where the former is when a war is declared under the laws of war.

1913 (no. 5543) and in the form of a map, no. B-44 published in 1914. In 1924, the map B-44 was republished as map no. 74. Both these maps are now known as 'the 1914 resolution' maps. It is also believed that the two maps are not similar but the resolution was implemented by placing pillars along the demarcated boundary line on land in 1924. The dispute resurrected in July 1948, after independence, when Pakistan raised the issue of delimitation of the Sindh-Kutch border that led to a war between the two countries in 1965. The dispute was referred to an arbitration panel subsequently. The panel published its decisions on February 19, 1968 defining a new boundary between Sindh and Kutch. Although Sir Creek was not within the purview of the panel, its award referred to the September 1913 document and thus created a link between the boundary defined by the panel and the boundary promulgated by the British in 1913. As per the directives of the panel, the two sides were to erect boundary pillars along the newly defined boundary, but the desired enthusiasm was lacking as there was implied reluctance in acceptance on the ground. This reluctance leading to 'no solution' as a solution is by default in strategic indecisiveness. The Sir Creek and other issues between the two countries are caught in this web with solutions dissolved in time. Though there were many meetings between the two countries, the issue is not yet resolved and is not likely to get demarcated for a very long time.[18]

In the meantime, the boundary disputes have created a virtual notional boundary line on either side of the proposed boundary lines which the trespassers should be aware of. It is an open boundary in reality. Through these notional limits, Indian and Pakistani fishers may enter each other's waters that can be established in spite of the dispute external to the notional line. The Indian Coast Guard (ICG) and its counterpart in Pakistan as well as the Maritime Security Agency (MSA) patrol the area close to the respective notional boundary lines. The trespassers are directed to leave the area if noticed within the notional limits. They get arrested if found further inside the territory. The problem here is social, political as well as technical and rests mainly in the resolution of the boundary. The problems will continue till then. Often, it is said, the fishers stealthily breach the lines to meet their

18. Prabhakaran Paleri, *Role of the Coast Guard in the Maritime Security of India,* 2nd ed. (New Delhi: KW Publishers Private Limited, 2007), pp. 99–102.

geographically separated families across the border. In this case, their chances of getting arrested by the security agencies increase. Most of the time, the fishers are repatriated as a goodwill gesture by both the countries.

The ICG and the MSA have been involved in regulating the fishers from trespassing across the notional boundary and also repatriating those arrested and released after diplomatic and legal intercourse. India and Pakistan had taken important and mature steps in regulating such trespassing. There is a memorandum of understanding to have regular contacts between the heads of the ICG and the MSA through visits and hotline communication. Such interactions help to diffuse volatile situations through confidence building. There are also active track 2 processes in building confidence between India and Pakistan.

The maritime relationship between India and Pakistan was left in a limbo when Pakistani-bred terrorists attacked India on November 26, 2008. They came by sea in a fishing boat across the disputed boundary.

As of today, both the countries hopefully seek technical resolution of the disputed boundary in Sir Creek estuary at the mouth of the Rann of Kutch in the Arabian Sea. In the meantime, they are conscious to contain the fisheries issues at the notional boundary.

The Maritime Border: Bangladesh–India

The maritime boundary between Bangladesh and India was under dispute for a very long time. Several rounds of talks have taken place since 1974. The problem was not so much political as technical. Bangladesh favoured an equitable solution whereas India favoured an equidistant line. The main dispute was over the sovereignty of the geologically unstable sandbar named South Talpatti or New Moore (Purbhasha) Island that emerged in 1971 in the wake of cyclonic activity in the area. It was approximately 5 km^2 in size at the mouth of Haribhanga River that marks the land boundary between the two countries. The island was first shown in the Admiralty Chart 859 by India. The Island disappeared in 2004 probably because of sea level rise.[19]

19. Ben Arnoldy, "Global Warming as Peacemaker? Disputed Island Disappears under Rising Sea," *The Christian Science Monitor* (March 2010). www.csmonitor.com/World/Asia-South-Central/2010/0324/Global-warming-as-peacemaker-Disputed-island-disappears-under-rising-sea.

India claimed the Haribhanga River flowed to the east of the Island whereas Bangladesh claimed it to be on the west. The dispute had more to do with the resources in the hydrocarbon-rich Ganges-Brahmaputra delta in the Bay of Bengal. There were voices in Bangladesh that India encroached Bangladeshi maritime zone violating international standards.[20] India also had experienced poaching in the waters of Sunderbans and adjacent waters on the Indian side. Sunderbans bordering Bay of Bengal spreads out into Bangladesh and India. It is the largest single block of tidal halophytic mangrove forest in the world. The delta harbours the entire ecosystem that acts as a nursery for the majority of fisheries species of Bay of Bengal. The Sunderbans is also the habitat of the famous Royal Bengal Tiger that has been declared an endangered species in 2010 by the International Union for the Conservation of Nature (IUCN).

The dispute between India and Bangladesh was resolved subsequent to an award by the Permanent Court of Attribution (PCA) of an area of 19,467 km^2 out of the total area of 25,602 remained disputed with India on July 7, 2014. Both the countries accepted the verdict as a positive development in Indo-Bangladesh maritime relations, and is expected to resolve various issues, including those related to the movement of fishers in the area.

In relation to the India-Pakistan maritime border, cross-border fishing at Bangladesh-India border is comparatively less. This can be attributed to the consumer taste for seafood, traditional practices in Bangladesh and the state of Bengal in India, more than the dispute. ICG had encountered large-scale poaching by alien trawlers other than Bangladeshis in the area in earlier times. This has been more or less eliminated by aggressive patrolling in the area. Poachers also used to move into the Sunderbans delta. There were also allegations that Bangladeshi fishers provide access to wildlife poachers in Sunderbans who target the Royal Bengal Tiger on the Indian side where its population is larger.

---

20. Abdullah Al Faruque, "Bangladesh-India Border Relations: A Truncated View," ndc.gov.bd/ elibrary/ webroot/ earticle/ 52/BD-India_Border_Relations.doc, accessed on August 3, 2013.

Findings

While the maritime dispute between India and Bangladesh stands resolved, lately, the long-standing problems between India and Pakistan are not likely to resolve in the near future. Dialogues may help to contain aggravation of the issues and associated flare-ups. India and Pakistan are considerably prudent and cautious in this matter. The issues are politically sensitive. It is expected that large amount of energy resources are available in the area. This will make the nations to approach the situation with extreme caution until they arrive at a solution that is judgmental or mutually beneficial. Considering there are various unresolved maritime disputes all over, some of them multilateral, the world will have to wait for long for amicable solutions that may perhaps set precedence for others to follow in a win-win situation. It will be a long wait. In the meantime, nations can carefully contain the issues. India and Pakistan have been treading carefully on this path. In the meantime, the collateral issues are manageable.

The November 26, 2008 attack on India from the sea subsequently came to be known as the 26/11 terror strike that involved the maritime boundary as well as a fishing trawler. It shows the porous nature of the boundary between India and Pakistan and the way fishing boats can be used to merge with the background in covert activities when there is neither an enforced fisheries regime nor a scientific vessel monitoring, control, surveillance and response system (MCSR) in force. The maritime borders between Bangladesh and India and other countries in South Asia are no different.

All the three countries have excellent marine fisheries potential, but have not been enthusiastic in exploiting them in a scientific way under international law and regulations for sustainability and export earnings. The issues in marine fisheries have not been catalysed by the disputed maritime borders seriously. The governments have been managing their disputed maritime borders more efficiently than their marine fisheries prospective. The two issues are seemingly detached. This is an important finding.

The three countries are highly populated in comparison with other countries of South Asia. They depend seriously on fisheries, including marine fisheries for food and economy. But marine fisheries or the sea is not in focus in their geostrategic relations that are ridden with conflicts.

Illegal and unreported fishing, the two elements of IUU fishing are predominant in Arabian Sea and Bay of Bengal. But there are no reports of alien poaching in India-Pakistan maritime border. However, there were occasional cases in the Bangladesh-India border in the earlier times. Presently, poaching in India and its maritime borders by alien vessels stand contained to a considerable extent by the efforts of the ICG which is a law enforcing force to reckon with in the area.

There are obvious problems with enforcing law in the territorial sea and the high sea of the exclusive economic zone. All the three countries need to modernise their fisheries and also introduce MCSR regimes in their respective areas individually or jointly. It will augur well for them.

Fisheries issues do not seriously contribute to the maritime border problems in the three countries with respect to the period of study. From the Indian perspective, the shadow falls from the problems over land. The governments may have to steer the maritime issues along with the land-based problems across borders. They could also be resolved locally by integrating maritime security with national security. The process is not examined in this article.

This study, though not inadvertently, runs into two issues—borders at sea and marine fisheries associated with it. But they both seem to have issues separate from each other and do not cause any collateral issues that would not have been there even if the boundaries were well demarcated and protected.

The three countries studied could do much more jointly for not only developing a disciplined and responsible fisheries management system in the South Asia maritime region but also maintaining a controlled ocean regime for safe and clean seas along with other members. The will somehow is lacking. This is the final finding.

Conclusion

While coastal waters of border zones are coastal controlled, the high seas could be better managed jointly by regional countries without trespassing into each other's jurisdiction. The three nations lose heavily on this in the absence of serious regional agreements. The disputed areas should be made into no fishing zones or joint fishing zones that may extend to the high seas. The countries should at least have joint agreements to exploit fisheries resources in a sustainable manner. They should endorse mandatory product certification and catch documentation jointly with the coastguards and corresponding agencies.

Among the eight South Asian countries (Afghanistan, Bangladesh, Bhutan, India, Maldives, Nepal, Pakistan and Sri Lanka), five have direct access to Indian Ocean. Though every nation in the world, whether coastal or landlocked, has the right to benefit from the ocean, the coastal nations have an obligatory privilege to protect and preserve the ocean for all. The South Asian maritime five (SAM5), therefore, need to assume a role different from others to safeguard the interests of all in South Asia by preparing to meet the challenges in the Indian Ocean by eliminating conflicts and maintaining tranquility jointly indifferent to their geopolitical differences for the common good. Perhaps South Asian Association for Regional Cooperation (SAARC) could review their protocol on ocean in this direction. India and Pakistan being the power-balancing forces in South Asia could take the lead to develop a regional regime for MCSR, maritime search and rescue, pollution response, disaster management along with the existing international obligations with vigour and spirit. This is seemingly an idealist gridlock, but can be opened under the faith of positive leadership that could see through populist politics.

According to the 2013 report of the United Nations, India along with Bhutan and Maldives are in the middle and Bangladesh as well as Pakistan at the low end of the human development index (HDI). Sri Lanka stands at the top in the high human development index. All these countries except Bhutan are coastal and could be the guardians of the ocean under an integrated and pragmatic regional ocean policy. However, it could be a long route to achieve it, looking at the perceptional differences among them on security. This trend can be damaging to the overall interests of the nations in the region.

Bibliography

"The World Bank, India Marine Fisheries, 2011," www.indiaenvironmentportal.org.in/files/file/India_ Marine_ fisheries.pdf, accessed on July 28, 2013.

Abdullah Al Faruque, "Bangladesh-India Border Relations: A Truncated View," ndc.gov.bd/elibrary/ webroot/ earticle/ 52/BD-India_Border_Relations.doc, accessed on August 3, 2013.

Ben Arnoldy, "Global Warming as Peacemaker? Disputed Island Disappears under Rising Sea," www.csmonitor.com/World/Asia-South-Central/2010/0324/Global-warming-as-peacemaker-Disputed-island-disappears-under-rising-sea, *The Christian Science Monitor* (March 2010). www.csmonitor.com/World/Asia-South-Central/2010/0324/Global-warming-as-peacemaker-Disputed-island-disappears-under-rising-sea, accessed on August 3, 2013.

Humayun Kabir, "Marine Fisheries in Bangladesh: an Overview," library.enaca.org/NACA-Publications/MaricultureWorkshop/MaricultureWS2006_Bangladesh.pdf, accessed on August 2, 2013.

John Heilprin, "Most Nations 'Ignore UN Fisheries Code," *The Sydney Morning Herald*, (February 2009). news.smh.com.au/breaking-news-world/most-nations-ignore-un-fisheries-code-20090205-7y2y.html, accessed on July 30, 2013.

Lisa Speer, "Marine Fisheries, Population and Consumption: Science and Policy Issues," (September 1995). www.aaas.org/ international/ehn/fisheries/speer.htm, accessed on July 28, 2013.

P. U. Zachaeria, "Present and Future Scenario of Indian Marine Fisheries," cmfri.org.in/uploads_en/divisions/files/Present%20and%20future%20scenario%20of%20Indfian%20marine%20fisheries.pdf, accessed on August 3, 2013.

Pakissan, "Agri overview: Fisheries sector in Pakistan," pakissan.com/english/ agri.overview/fisheries.sector.in.pakistan.shtml, and "Brief on Environmental Problems of the Marine and Coastal Areas," www.environment.gov.pk/PRO_PDF/PositionPaper/Marine%20pollution.pdf, accessed 2 August 2, 2013.

Prabhakaran Paleri, *Coast Guards of the World and Emerging Maritime Threats* (Tokyo: Ocean Policy Research Foundation, 2009).

——, *Marine Environment: Management and People's Participation* (New Delhi: KW Publishers Private Limited, 2009).

——, *Maritime Security: the Unlawful Dimension* (New Delhi: Magnum Books Private Limited, 2010).

——, *Role of the Coast Guard in the Maritime Security of India* (New Delhi: KW Publishers Private Limited, 2007).

The Indian Express Team, *Inside 26/11* (New Delhi: Rupa and Company, 2009).

6. Seaborne Illegal Migration from South Asia to Australia

A Sri Lankan Perspective

Saman Jayawickrama

The term 'migration', especially in the Third World countries, generally reflects as an avenue to escape from relative poverty and it is further a movement by people from one geographical location to another with intentions of settling temporarily or permanently with the main aim of better prospects of a livelihood. The movement is often over long distances and from one country to another, but internal migration that implies within the border of a particular country is also possible; indeed, this is the dominant form globally. Migration may close the window of opportunities pushing individuals and communities into new social and political spaces where their previous social structure and economic network cannot support and protect them.

With the inception of open economy, easy flow of funds and investments across the borders introduced many avenues and opportunities to citizens. People were exposed to a new world with more comforts and luxuries which are in monetary term beyond their reach. These new-found luxuries are for the use of a particular segment of people who can afford it. Thus, an economical demarcation and financial segmentation within the population built up within no time. Globalisation which is hand in hand with open economy created further uneven economic segregations. Darker side of globalisation is disparities of income, different structure of labour and supply conditions and so forth, which were a greater threat for the safety and stability of a country's economy and affect the gross domestic product (GDP).[1] However, if a country's economy is stagnated within a certain class of population, leaving behind a large number of populations fighting to meet their day-to-day needs, then there is a greater risk for these less fortunate, vulnerable individuals or rather communities. They are a group which is exposed and becomes an easy target for deception and exploitation by traffickers and agents, and subsequently it is a very big threat to the state security. Marginalised rural families due to lack of education and exposure to the threats awaiting them in a form of sugar-coated pill were easy targets for these agents and traffickers.

With regard to illegal migration, it generally occurs when people migrate across borders without authorised legal documents. It may occur due to some highly emotive issues, such as terrorism, people trafficking, prostitution, child abuse, asylum-seeking, illegal employment and growth of under classes. Illegal migration is overwhelmingly upwards from a poorer to a richer country depending upon the quality of life in the host country against the home country.

Trends/Causes

Illegal migration occurs principally from countries with lower socio-economic circumstances to countries with higher socio-economic circumstances, where people are perceived to have greater economic opportunities and quality of life. When potential migrants believe the probability and benefits of successfully migrating to the destination country are greater than the costs,[2] illegal migration becomes an option. The benefits taken into account include not only expected improvements in the income and living conditions but also expectations in relation to potential future residential permits where undocumented migrants are given a path to naturalisation or citizenship.

1. Gross domestic product (GDP) is the broadest quantitative measure of a nation's total economic activity. More specifically, GDP represents the monetary value of all goods and services produced within a nation's geographic borders over a specified period of time.
2. The costs may include restrictions on living as an illegal immigrant in the destination country, leaving family and ways of life behind and the probability of being detained and resulting sanctions.

Seaborne Illegal Migration

General understanding of seaborne illegal migration is people who illegally transfer from one destination to another via sea by means of seaborne vessels.[3]

South Asia (Indian Ocean Region [IOR])

South Asian region which currently signifies as Indian Ocean Region (IOR) is home to well over one fifth of the world's population, making it both the most populous and the most densely populated geographical region in the world. The countries which make up the South Asian region are Afghanistan, Bangladesh, Bhutan, India, Maldives, Pakistan, Nepal and Sri Lanka. Sometimes, Myanmar is also included as it is linked by the South Asian Association for Regional Cooperation (SAARC). The region is ethnically diverse, with more than 2,000 ethnic entities with populations ranging from hundreds of millions to small tribal groups. IOR, the birthplace of maritime civilisation, was considered a playground of rich industrial European nations during the colonial era.

With the commencement of decolonisation in 1946, the euphoria of independence was overshadowed by the turbulence of internecine conflicts and interstate wars that followed. During the Cold War era, the two superpowers reinforced their maritime influence directly or indirectly through an impressive array of available port facilities in this region. The post-Cold War era has heralded a socio-politico-strategic shift in thought. Globalisation, specifically economics, today dominates strategic considerations. This has led to enhanced maritime security concerns, as most regional trade is seaborne. Despite 'maritime bonding', this region has unfortunately not seen the emergence of a vibrant transoceanic community. This may be rooted in regional countries 'wide dissimilarities and divergent interests' which have prompted each country to pursue economic linkages with Europe or North America rather than with each other. This has inevitably limited the region's economic growth.

3. Source: Article 3 of the Regulations of Temporary Entry Permit for Foreigners: National Immigration Agency, Ministry of Interior, 14/01/13 (viewed on 03/09/13: web ref: http://iff.immigration.gov)

IOR is the poorest region in the world after sub-Saharan Africa. According to UN's Multidimensional Poverty Index[4] (MPI), just over a quarter of the world's MPI poor people live in Africa, while a half lives in South Asia. According to the World Bank, 70 percent of the South Asian population and about 75 percent of South Asia's poor live in rural areas and most rely on agriculture for their livelihood. According to the Global Hunger Index (GHI),[5] South Asia has one of the highest child malnutrition rates in the world. In a latest report published by UNICEF,[6] in 2008, on global hunger shows that the actual number of child deaths was around 2.1 million. As of 2008, India ranked 66th on the GHI. The 2006 report stated that 'low status of women in South Asian countries and their lack of nutritional knowledge are important determinants of high prevalence of underweight children in the region'. The report mentioned that, although there has been a reduction in malnutrition due to the Green Revolution in South Asia,[7] there is concern that South Asia has 'inadequate feeding and caring practices for young children'.

4. The **Multidimensional Poverty Index (MPI)** was developed in 2010 by Oxford Poverty & Human Development Initiative and the United Nations Development Programme and uses different factors to determine poverty beyond income-based lists. It replaced the previous Human Poverty Index. The MPI is an index of acute multidimensional poverty. It shows the number of people who are multidimensionally poor (suffering deprivations in 33.33 percent of weighted indicators) and the number of deprivations with which poor households typically contend. It reflects deprivations in very rudimentary services and core human functioning for people across 104 countries. Although deeply constrained by data limitations, MPI reveals a different pattern of poverty than income poverty, as it illuminates a different set of deprivations.
5. The **Global Hunger Index (GHI)** is a multidimensional statistical tool used to describe the state of countries' hunger situation. The GHI measures progress and failures in the global fight against hunger. The GHI is updated once a year.
6. The United Nations International Children's Emergency Fund or UNICEF is now known as the United Nation's Children Fund and it was founded in order to help the children of war-torn countries. Source: UNICEF Home Page at www.unicef.org accessed on September 15, 2013.
7. An increase in food production, especially in underdeveloped and developing nations, is through the introduction of high-yield crop varieties and application of modern agricultural techniques. The introduction of high-yielding varieties of seeds and the increased use of chemical fertilizers and irrigation are known collectively as the Green Revolution, which provided the increase in production needed to make South Asia self-sufficient in food grains, thus improving agriculture in South Asia.

Sri Lanka

Sri Lanka is a democratic republic and an unitary state which is governed by both a presidential and parliamentary system. Sri Lanka[8] became a member of the United Nations in 1955. From a Sri Lankan perspective, illegal migration is committed mainly for socio-economic reasons. Geographical location of the country is one of the prominent reasons for the rise in human trafficking during the past decades. In terms of the Sri Lankan asylum seekers in Australia, one dominant question seems to pop up over and over again. Why, when a 26-year old conflict that caused so many to leave their homes has ended, do more and more Sri Lankan refugees continue to make the dangerous journey to Australia on an unseaworthy vessel? As one might imagine, the answer is not a simple one and goes both to the history of the conflict and Sri Lanka's road to peace. In 2009, though the 30 years long Sri Lankan civil war ended with the government forcing a complete defeat for the independence struggle of the Tamil Tigers (known as Liberation Tigers of Tamil Eelam (LTTE)), human traffic is still a major issue the government facing. The end of violence evoked both hope and apprehension on all sides: on one hand, there was the promise of a new era that could draw on the great natural riches of the country and on the other; there was uncertainty about whether all parties could coexist peacefully in the future, working towards a common goal with their differentiations in the political vision.

Australia

Australia, officially the Commonwealth of Australia, is the world's sixth largest country by total area and is a highly developed country, though it too is a British colony. The country possesses the world's 12th largest economy and has the world's fifth highest per capita

8. Sri Lanka is also a member of the Commonwealth, the SAARC, World Bank, International Monetary Fund, Asian Development Bank and the Colombo Plan. The country has had a long history of international engagement, being a founding member of SAARC and a member of the United Nations, the Commonwealth of Nations, the G77 and the Non-Aligned Movement. It is also the only country in South Asia that is currently rated 'high' on the Human Development Index.

income. Australia's military expenditure is the world's 13th largest. With the second highest human development index globally, Australia ranks high in many international comparisons of national performance, such as the quality of life, health, education, economic freedom and the protection of civil liberties as well as political rights. People smuggling and trafficking in persons are serious transnational crimes that require a concerted regional response. Smuggling people exposes many thousands of illegal migrants to unacceptable risks and undermines the integrity of Sri Lankan and Australian borders. Trafficking in persons is a complex, multifaceted crime and a major violation of human rights. Australia seeks to address these issues by working bilaterally with source, transit and destination countries and multilaterally through the Bali Process[9] on People Smuggling, Trafficking in Persons and Related Transnational Crime (the Bali Process), which Australia co-founded and co-chairs with Indonesia. Since its inception in 2002, the Bali Process has raised regional awareness of the consequences of people smuggling and trafficking in persons and developed strategies and practical cooperative measures in response.

Three types[10] of migration from and within IOR are:

- permanent migration to Europe, Australia, and North America;
- contract labour migration to the Gulf States and South East Asia and
- Cross-border and seasonal migration within the region.

A journal article on seaborne illegal migration published by journalists for democracy in Sri Lanka under the heading 'Sri Lankan boat migration to Australia: Motivations and Dilemmas', published on September 1, 2013

---

9. The Bali Process is a regional, multilateral process designed to boost bilateral and regional cooperative efforts against people smuggling and trafficking in persons through technical workshops and increased cooperation between interested countries, the Office of the United Nations High Commissioner for Refugees (UNHCR) and International Organisation for Migration (IOM). Overall direction and coordination of the Bali Process is provided through an officials' level Steering Group comprising Indonesia and Australia as the two co-chairs, New Zealand, Thailand, UNHCR and IOM.
10. Source: World Bank's Migration and Remittances Fact book, 2008 and 2007.

Figure 6.1: Seaborne Illegal Migration in the IOR

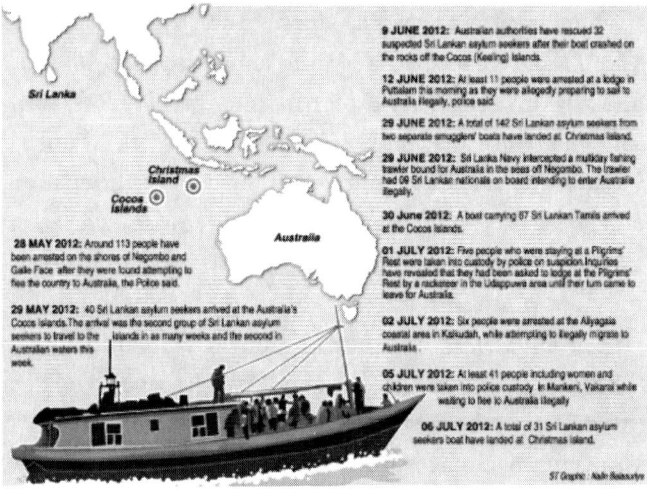

Source: Google image extracted from website reference: https://www.google.lk (visited the site on September 4, 2013.

says, "in 2012, a record 6,412 Sri Lankan people made journey by boat to Australia (boat migrants) without passing through an official Sri Lankan port, including over 1,000 Sinhala people." In the same year, Sri Lankan authorities claim to have intercepted over 3,000 Sri Lankans en route to Australia. The numbers continued to rise in 2013 with over 1,730 Sri Lankans arriving in Australia in July.[11] This is a record number of Sri Lankan migrants in Australia. Even during 2009, at the end of Sri Lanka's civil war, Australia received only 736 Sri Lankan boat migrants.[12] During 2011 only 211 Sri Lankans arrived in Australia by boat. For the first time in 2012, Sri Lankans comprised the biggest single national group among boat arrivals in Australia, this was also the year in which Australia received the largest number of boats on record. During the same period, asylum applications from Sri Lankans dropped in Canada, France, Germany, United Kingdom and United States. Four years after the end of Sri Lanka's civil war, it is difficult to pinpoint what has caused this sudden and exponential surge in boat migrants to Australia.

11. Source: Emily Howie, "Sri Lankan Boat Migration to Australia: Motivations and Dilemmas", *Economic and Political Weekly: Special Article,* vol. 48, no. 35, 2013.
12. Source: UNHCR 2012b.

Why has Australia arisen as the most popular destination for Sri Lankan boat migrants, if anyone believes the rhetoric of governments, the boats are full of 'economic migrants' simply seeking jobs and higher living standards in Australia. According to Sri Lanka's former high commissioner to Australia, retired Naval Chief of Sri Lanka Admiral Thisara Samarasinghe, boat migrants are not fleeing persecution, but are economic opportunists seeking a better life.[13] Likewise, Sri Lanka's former minister for external affairs, Mr G. L. Peris, opined that boat migrants are "certainly not political refugees because there is nothing to run away from."[14] The Australian Government, managing competing electoral, legal and moral imperatives to stop the boats arriving, while complying (or at least wishing to be seen to comply) with its obligations under the Refugee Convention, has been only slightly less emphatic. Then Australian minister for foreign affairs, Senator Bob Carr, said in relation to all boat arrivals in Australia that they are all or primarily economic.[15] Jose Alvarez, Australian immigration's South Asia director, described Sri Lankan boat migrants as 'economic refugees', saying that the majority of Sri Lankan boat migrants arriving in Australia from Sri Lanka had economic reasons for their journey.[16] The claims of Carr and Alvarez have no basis in relation to Sri Lankan boat migrants. An overwhelming majority of Sri Lankan boat migrants have claimed asylum on arrival in Australia and none of the people who arrived after August 2012 have had their claims processed.[17] Historically, 90 percent of boat arrivals in Australia are found to be refugees.[18]

13. Sri Lankan High Commissioner to Australia, Admiral Samarasinghe, stated "The people are fleeing not because of leaving the shores, not because of any persecution; there are economic opportunities coming to Australia for a better life", ABC Late line (April 10, 2013). http://www.abc.net.au, accessed on August 11, 2013.
14. Source: Richardson 2013.
15. See Bob Carr's comments on ABC Late line (June 28, 2013). http://www.abc.net.au, viewed on 29/08/13.
16. Source: Alvarez 2012.
17. Source: Hall 2013, Martin Bowles, Secretary to DIAC during questioning in Senate Estimates, May 27, 2013, reported in Hall (2013).
18. Source: Department of Immigration and Citizenship statistics, reported in Hall (2013b).

Figure 6.2: Sri Lankan Sailors Rescue 138 Stranded on Sinking boat

(Source: Google Image on title, 'Lanka Sailors rescue 138 stranded on sinking boat' extracted from website: www.gulf-times.com on 05/09/13).

Australia forcibly returns Sri Lankans for apparently failing to articulate a refugee or broader complementary protection claim upon arrival. Critics point out that the returnees do not have a proper refugee status determination and that the assessment process they faced is secret, truncated, with the applicant having no access to lawyers and the decision to deport them not subject to review.[19] Most of these boat migrants may be taking this decision to leave the safety of their homeland purely economic reasons, but it is simply cannot discount the numbers of refugees among the boat migrants or to assert any empirical or evidential basis for doing so. The motivations for boat migration do not always arise from fears for personal safety and security. Tamil-majority areas in the north and east that creates livelihood challenges and a sense of frustration, hopelessness and despair about any possible change in the near future are few reasons for that. Fishermen who tried to leave Sri Lanka on boats speak about the injustice of the 'pass system' for fishing and the incursion of Sinhala and Indian fishermen in local waters.

Some Tamil fishermen complained that although they are allowed to fish, they are unable to fish for the more lucrative catches, such as sea

19. Source: HRLC 2013 during 2013/14, using our strategic combination of legal action, advocacy, research and capacity building, addressed the UN's Human Rights Council on how Australia's asylum seeker policies violate the international law.

cucumbers, because they could not obtain a permit that enabled them to use an oxygen tank (or cylinder), while fishing. Others in the Northern Province expressed their worries and frustration at the use of their traditional fishing grounds by Sinhalese and Indian fishermen, with no protection of the fishing areas by the state and limited financial means to compete, they think their future is at a risk. But 'How do we stop this from happening?' is not such a simple question. To answer it, you first need to answer another question: 'Why are these people taking such risks?' And it's worth asking a third, often ignored question, as well: Why has illegal-boat migration to Australia peaked during last couple of years, and what will make it stop?

Border Security in Sri Lanka

It is a violation of Sri Lanka's immigration law to leave the country without documents in order and other than from an official port. Boat migrants who are caught by the Sri Lankan authorities when they tried to leave Sri Lanka are taken into custody and charged with illegal migration under the Sri Lankan law. Most are granted bail, but those who are suspected of facilitating the operations are remanded and prosecuted for a certain period of prison sentence.

Paradigm of Economic Migration

In Australia, the arrival of record numbers of asylum-seekers by boat become a political catastrophe that threatens to bring down the ruling government in national elections. The 2001 Australian federal election is widely believed to have been won by the then Howard Government on the back of its seizing of the M. V. Tampa, a Norwegian freighter that had rescued 400 asylum-seekers at sea, and the subsequent implementation of the Pacific solution in which new arrivals were sent offshore for processing in Pacific islands.

Since 2012, however, boats began to arrive in large numbers; the Australian Government reintroduced the Pacific solution, a policy which was abandoned nearly five years ago. Australia's border security cooperation with Sri Lanka to stop boats before they leave is seen by the Australian Government as a key plank in slowing the number of boat arrivals. In terms of Australia and Sri Lanka's bilateral relations, it has emerged as the pre-eminent, if not the primary concern. Australia has become increasingly reluctant to engage critically with Sri Lanka on human rights issues for fear of jeopardizing the strategic border security partnership. The change can be seen over the past year or so. In March 2012 Australia co-sponsored the United Nations Human Rights Council[20] (UNHRC) resolution calling on Sri Lanka to address allegations of war crimes at the end of the civil war.[21]

Conclusion

It is not only Sri Lankan's who tends to illegal migration. There are millions of others from Tunis, Alexandria; Marseilles, Munich ..., etc., have now become Europe's biggest concern. There is evidence that ex-LTTE cadres have come to Australia, in the past, Earlier, laws calling for up to 20 years of prison term for people smuggling had been introduced in the Australian Parliament. It is not only were Sri Lankans trying to illegally leave the country but also foreigners such as Pakistanis and Afghan nationals who use Sri Lanka as a transit point. The flow of refugees commonly increases, not decreases, after the end of a conflict. This happened after the wars in Vietnam and Bosnia-Herzegovina, after conflicts across Africa and South America, and even after the First and Second World Wars. The million or so people who left South-east Asia after the wars in Vietnam, Cambodia and Laos were not fleeing straightforward oppression: they were leaving behind sites of trauma and despair that had become too painful. Illegal migrants are an unnecessary social problem to any country. It is the border controls which tighten day by day which forced them to take more dangerous routes while sacrificing their hard earned or perhaps sometimes borrowed sum of rupees for cross border smugglers. Fast growing economies with virtually unemployment are another major driving force for people to cross the boarders as illegal migrants. The flight of Sri Lankan citizens Tamil, Sinhala and Muslim after

20. The Human Rights Council is an intergovernmental body within the United Nations system made up of 47 States responsible for the promotion and protection of all human rights around the globe. Source: UNHCR website, http://www.ohchr.org, accessed on September 15, 2013.
21. Source: Department of Foreign Affairs and Trade Country Brief on Sri Lanka, http://www.dfat.gov.au accessed on August 30, 2013.

the conclusion of the recent civil war largely fits this pattern. Thousands of people are prepared to risk their lives to leave the safety of their homeland as they do not see a future for themselves. Therefore they leave because their hope, depleted by decades of conflict, has not been restored by the cessation of hostilities and the restoration of some level of material wealth. To build confidence in a shared future requires careful and deliberate action across all levels of government and civil society. Sri Lanka today is a place of promise, but also with dire challenges. The fighting may have stopped but the work of reconstruction and reconciliation needs to be well-coordinated. It is now evident that boat migrants risk their lives their comfort for a journey that at best promise a more socio economically sound livelihood in the hosting country. Provision of material wealth and the proliferation of commodities are not in themselves sufficient to create confidence in the future. The ending of a war does not automatically resolve the conflict that precipitated it. Availability of the bare material goods does not recreate a sense of purpose and value or fill the void of meaning. These things can be achieved only by drawing together the disparate communities in a spirit of mutual forgiveness where the current political regime attempting to initiate which gives a promise to its citizen. However it is time for Sri Lanka to allow itself the possibility of moving along such a path to reconciliation and for the international community to support it in doing so. The end of the conflict has opened a window of opportunity that must not be lost, current regime of the country is working towards more sustainable infrastructure planning for the needs of its populace. However, it is evenly a mandatory policy decision if a set of more vital and materialistic planning is not implemented, socio-economic imbalance will definitely leave thousands of bodies floating in the sea in years to come.

Bibliography

A. K. M. Masud Ali, "Treading along a Treacherous Trail: Research on Trafficking in Persons in South Asia". Data and Research on Human Trafficking: A Global Survey (Geneva: IOM, 2005).

Abrar Chowdhury, "Patterns of Migration of South Asians to the Gulf Region: Their Main Problems and Issues" (seminar presentation on Labour Migration, Employment and Poverty Alleviation in South Asia, Kathmandu, August 9–10, 2007).

Amnesty International, "*Australians Support Equal Rights for Asylum Seekers*" (August 12, 2009), http://www.amnesty.org.au, accessed on September 23, 2013.

Amnesty International, "*Manus and 'No Advantage' Announcement Squib Refugee Protection*," Media release (October, 21, 2012). http://www.amnesty.org.au, accessed on September 24, 2013.

Andrew Markus and Rebeca Raijman, "Immigration and public opinion," in Andrew Markus, ed., *Immigration and nation building: Australia and Israel compared* (Cheltenham: Edward Elgar Publishing, 2010), pp. 115–140.

Andrew Markus, *Mapping Social Cohesion 2010* (Monash: Monash Institute for the Study of Global Movements, 2010), p. 39.

Anne Gallagher, "Human Rights and the New UN Protocols on Trafficking and Migrant Smuggling: A Preliminary Analysis," *Human Rights Quarterly*, vol. 23, no. 4, 2001, pp. 975–1004.

Asian Development Bank, *Education and National Development in Asia: Trends, Issues, Policies, and Strategies* (Manila: ADB, 2001).

Athula Ranasinghe, "Remittance Economy and its Contribution to Poverty Alleviation in South Asia: A Case Study of Sri Lanka" (seminar presentation on Labour Migration, Employment and Poverty Alleviation in South Asia, Kathmandu, Nepal, August 9–10, 2007).

Ben Doherty, "Hard Line Asylum Stance Won't Stop Them Leaving, but It May Stop Them Arriving," *Sydney Morning Herald*, (July 20, 2013a). http://www.smh.com.au, accessed on August 29, 2013.

Bridget Anderson and Julia O'Connell Davidson, *Is Trafficking in Human Beings Demand Driven: A Multi-Country Pilot Study* (Geneva: IOM, 2003).

Chandra Rodrigo, "Overseas Migration from Sri Lanka: Magnitude, Patterns and Trends." *Asian Exchange* vol. 8, no. 3/4, pp. 41–74.

Chris Evans (Minister for Immigration and Citizenship), "*Government to Move Children and Vulnerable Families into Community-Based Accommodation,*" Media release, Canberra (October 18, 2010), http://www.minister.immi.gov.au, accessed on August 23, 2013.

Chris Evans (Minister for Immigration and Citizenship), "*Last refugees leave Nauru,*" media release, Canberra, (February 8, 2008), http://parlinfo.aph.gov.au, accessed on August 23, 2013.

Christopher Bowen (Minister for Immigration and Citizenship), "*Additional Immigration Detention Accommodation,*" Media release, Canberra (September 17, 2010), http://www.minister.immi.gov.au, accessed on August 23, 2013.

Claire Brolan, "An Analysis of the Human Smuggling Trade and the Protocol against the Smuggling of Migrants by Land, Air or Sea (2000) from a Refugee Protection Perspective," *International Journal of Refugee Law*, 14, no. 4, 2002, pp. 561–596.

Dan Flitton, "Sri Lankan Navy Thwarts Refugees", *The Age* (September 15, 2011). http://m.theage.com.au.

Daniel Flitton, "Tamil Refugee was Child Soldier Trainer," *The Age* (September 6, 2013). http://www.theage.com.au/federal-politics/federal-election-2013/tamil-refugee-was-child-soldier-trainer-20130905-2t84h.html, accessed on January 1, 2016.

David Richardson, "Sri Lanka Fights Smugglers," *Today Tonight* (March 26, 2013). http://au.news.yahoo.com, accessed on August 14, 2013.

Department of Immigration and Ethnic Affairs, *Review '83* (Canberra: Australian Government Publishing Service, 1983), p. 31.

DIAC, *"Australia's Refugee and Humanitarian Program,"* Fact sheet no. 60, http://www.immi.gov.au, accessed on August 23, 2013.

DIAC, *"Australia's Refugee and Humanitarian Program,"* Fact sheet no. 60, http://www.immi.gov.au, accessed on August 23, 2013.

DIAC, *"Over Stayers and Other Unlawful Non-Citizens,"* Fact sheet no. 86, http://www.immi.gov.au, accessed on August 23, 2013.

DIAC, *"Processing Unlawful Boat Arrivals,"* Fact sheet no. 75, http://www.immi.gov.au, accessed on August 11, 2013.

DIAC, *"Seeking Asylum within Australia,"* Fact sheet no. 61, http://www.immi.gov.au, accessed on August 23, 2013.

Economic Times, "The Various Issues," New Delhi.

Emily Howie, "Sri Lankan Boat Migration to Australia: Motivations and Dilemmas", *Economic and Political weekly: Special Article,* vol. 48, no. 35, 2013, pp. 97–104. http://www.epw.in/system/files/pdf/2013_48/35/Sri_Lankan_Boat_Migration_to_Australia.pdf, accessed on January 1, 2016.

Eric Richards, *Destination Australia: Migration to Australia since 1901* (Sydney: University of New South Wales Press, 2008), p. 263.

Expert Panel on Asylum Seekers (A Houston, chair), *"Report of the Expert Panel on Asylum Seekers,"* Australian Government, Canberra (August 2012). http://expertpanelonasylumseekers.dpmc.gov.au, accessed on August 22, 2013.

Fergus Hanson, *Lowy Institute Poll 2010 Australia and the world: public opinion and foreign policy*, Lowy Institute for International Policy, 2010, p. 3.

Ganesh Gurung, Patterns in Foreign Employment and Vulnerability of Migrant Workers (Kathmandu: Nepal Institute of Development Studies, 2000), http:// www.childtrafficking.com, accessed on August 6, 2013.

Gerry Hand, 'Second reading speech: Migration Reform Bill 1992', House of Representatives, *Debates*, November 4, 1992, p. 2620.

Global Migration Group, "International migration and human rights—Challenges and Opportunities on the threshold of the 60th Anniversary of the Universal Declaration of Human Rights," October 2008, pp. 25–26.

Haris Gazdar, Hussain Bux Mullah and Rashid Memon. *Irregular Migration and Non-Traditional Threats to State Security: The Case of Karachi* (Dhaka: Refugee and Migratory Movements Research Unit, 2005).

Human Rights and Equal Opportunity Commission, "Those Who've Come across the Seas: Detention of Unauthorized Arrivals," Commonwealth of Australia (May 1998). http://www.hreoc.gov.au, accessed on August 23, 1998.

ILO, *Migrant Workers and Human Rights: Out-Migration from South Asia* (Geneva: ILO, 2004).

IOM (International Organization for Migration), *World Migration 2005: Costs and Benefits of International Migration* (Geneva: IOM, 2005).

"Irregular Migration, Migrant Smuggling and Human Rights: Towards Coherence," *International Council on Human Rights Policy* (2010). http://www.ichrp.org, accessed on August 5, 2013.

Jagannath Adhikari, Comments from the floor on Athula Ranasinghe's paper, "Remittance Economy and its contribution to poverty alleviation in South Asia: A Case Study of Sri Lanka" (seminar presentation on Labour Migration, Employment and Poverty Alleviation in South Asia, Kathmandu, August 9–10, 2007a).

Janet Phillips and Harriet Spinks, "Boat Arrivals in Australia since 1976," Parliament of Australia (updated January 29, 2013). http://www.aph.gov.au, accessed on August 11, 2013.

Jennifer Van Hook, Frank Bean and Jeffrey Passel, "Unauthorized Migrants Living in the United States: A Mid-Decade Portrait," *Migration Information Source* (2005), http://www.migrationinformation.org, accessed on August 23, 2013.

John Howard (Prime Minister), *"Immigration detention,"* Media release, Canberra (May 17, 2005). http://parlinfo.aph.gov.au, accessed on August 23, 2013.

Julia Gillard (Prime Minister) and John C. Bowen (Minister for Immigration and Citizenship), *"Transcript of joint press conference,"* Media release, Canberra (October 13, 2011). http://parlinfo.aph.gov.au, accessed on August 18, 2013.

Laura Maria Agustín, "Forget Victimization: Granting Agency to Migrants," *Society for International Development,* vol. 46, no. 3, 2003, pp. 30–36, www.sidint.org.

Madhukar Rana, Comments from the floor on Athula Ranasinghe's paper "Remittance Economy and Its Contribution to Poverty Alleviation in South Asia: A Case Study of Sri Lanka" (seminar presentation on Labour Migration, Employment and Poverty Alleviation in South Asia, Kathmandu, Nepal, August 9–10, 2007).

Manolo Abella and Geoffrey Ducanes, Technical Note: the effect of the global economic crisis on Asian migrant workers and governments' responses (Bangkok: ILO Regional Office for Asia and the Pacific, 2009).

Migration in an Interconnected World: New Direction for Action. http://www.gcim.org, accessed on August 10, 2013.

Muttukrishna Sarvananthan, "Sri Lanka: Putting Entrepreneurship at the Heart of Economic Revival in the North, East, and Beyond," *Contemporary South Asia,* vol. 19, no. 2, 2011, pp. 205-213. http://www.tandfonline.com/doi/abs/10.1080/09584935.2011.565313, accessed on January 2, 2016.

Nancy Viviani, *The long journey: Vietnamese migration and settlement in Australia* (Carlton: Melbourne University Press, 1984), p. 79.

Nazish Brohi and Zia Ahmad Awan, *Shattered Dreams and Living Nightmares: Situational Analysis on Trafficking of Women and Children in Pakistan* (Rawalpidi: Action Aid Pakistan, 2000).

Nirmala Kannangara, "Tales of Udappuwa Asylum Seekers," *Sunday Leader* (September 23, 2012). http://www.thesundayleader.lk, accessed on August 13, 2013.

P. C. Rodrigo, "Migration for Employment Overseas: Some Dimensions of the Sri Lankan Experience." In *Annual Bulletin of Research Institute for Social Science,* No. 27/03/97, 1997.

Paula Banerjee, "Women Trafficking and Statelessness in South Asia," *Refugee Watch* no. 27, 2006, pp. 74–93.

Peter Browne, "Boats and Votes: More Evidence on the Opinion Gap," *Inside Story,* online only (June 16, 2010). http://inside.org.au, accessed on August 23, 2013.

Rachel Ball, "'Screening out' Asylum Seekers Undermines Rule of Law and Risks Returning People to Face Torture", *Human Rights Law Centre* (December 20, 2012). http://www.hrlc.org.au, accessed on August 15, 2013.

Richard Adams, Jr. "Remittances, Investment and Rural Asset Accumulation in Pakistan," *Economic Development and Cultural Change,* vol. 47, no. 1, pp. 155–173.

Richard Black, "Migration, Globalization and Poverty: The New DFID-Funded Development Research Centre on Migration." (Department for International

Development ASREP-SLSO Lunchtime Seminar, London, February 24, 2003). www.livelihoods.org, accessed on August 14, 2013.

Sergie De Silva Ranasinghe, "Bitterness Towards the LTTE has not Translated into Goodwill towards the Government," *The Sunday Leader* (November 14, 2010). http://www.thesundayleader.lk/?p=27596, accessed on January 6, 2016.

Siri Gamage, "Curtains of Culture, Ethnicity and Class: The Changing Composition of the Sri Lankan Community in Australia," *Journal of Intercultural Studies,* vol. 19, no. 1, pp. 37–56.

Sri Lanka Bureau of Foreign Employment, *Statistical Handbook on Foreign Employment,* Colombo, 2006.

Tapan Bose, *Protection of Refugees in South Asia: Need for Legal Framework* (Kathmandu: South Asia Forum for Human Rights, 2000).

Tim Dyson, Twenty-first Century India: Population, Economy, Human Development, and the Environment, eds., Tim Dyson, Robert Cassen and Leela Visaria (Delhi: Oxford University Press, 2004).

UNHCR, "2009 Global Trends: Refugees, Asylum-Seekers, Returnees, Internally Displaced and Stateless Persons," *UNHCR* (June 2010), p. 2. http://www.unhcr.org, accessed on August 23, 2013.

UNHCR, "All in the Same Boat: The Challenges of Mixed Migration," UNHCR website, http://www.unhcr.org, accessed on August 3, 2013.

UNHCR, "Asylum Levels and Trends in Industrialized Countries 2008," *UNHCR,* (March 2009), p. 3, accessed on http://www.unhcr.org, accessed on August 23, 2013.

UNODC report, "Smuggling Migrants of South Asia," http://www.unodc.org, accessed on August 1, 2013.

7. Illegal Migration from South Asia to Australia

An Analysis of Australia's Response

Ananda Weerasinghe and *Mahinda Attanayake*

Introduction

As a country founded mainly by overseas settlers, inward migration has been a major contributory factor to Australia's nation-building. The country's national anthem proudly professes the value of migration in the following lines

For those who've come across the seas
We've boundless plains to share,
With courage let us all combine
To advance Australia fair

Although this reflects the views of the forefathers, due to the threat of Chinese migration and more recently due to hordes of illegal maritime arrivals especially from South and South East Asia, and due to international security concerns in the post-9/11 era, the country has gradually turned towards a strictly regulated restrictive approach towards migration and the question of illegal migration.

The development and strict adherence to the 'White Australia' policy that allowed only settlers with European ethnicity was the manifestation of the fears of ethnic domination by Chinese migrants. Even after the dismantling of this policy, Australia continued its preference for European settlers even by recruiting would—be settlers from the United Kingdom.

A new situation arose in the 1970s when illegal migrants consisting of 'Boat People' from politically unstable South East Asia, mainly Vietnam, ventured across rough seas in heavily loaded dilapidated boats. Although it was illegal migration, Australian Government and the public perceived it as refugees fleeing from political oppression and most of them were allowed in.

At present, Australia's illegal migration is reported to be mainly a people smuggling operation from assembly points in South Asia that sends boatloads of people across Indonesian waters to the closely situated Australian territory. The hinterland that supplies the potential illegal migrants includes the hot spots of international terrorist activities in the Middle East, that is, Iran, Iraq and Yemen, and so forth. It is believed that the money collected by the people-smugglers enrich the coffers of groups linked to international terrorism. Thus, the South Asian people smuggler's connections with terrorist groups and the very high possibility of their infiltration into groups of illegal migrants have generated legitimate concerns for Australia's national security and international reputation.

Although headline grabbing instances of human tragedies involving illegal migrants have occurred recently, the Australian public opinion and the political will has hardened against this form of illegal migration over the past two decades. The hard line came into being in the early 1990s with the introduction of mandatory detention of all illegal migrants. Invariably it has become a hot political issue in the Australian national elections.

The so-called Pacific Solution, by which Australia sought an arrangement with Australia's friendly neighbours in the tropical areas of the Pacific to accept the illegal immigrants until they were processed with the proviso of granting settlement in their respective countries for the most deserving of relocation, was a response to the events of August 2001 when 433 asylum seekers en route to Australia were rescued from their sinking vessel by the Norwegian freighter, 'MV Tampa' and delivered to Australia under maritime law. The asylum seekers were subsequently transferred to an Australian Navy ship and sent to the Pacific island of Nauru.

The decision of Kevin Rudd-led government, on the eve of September 2013 general elections, to negotiate an arrangement with Papua New Guinea (PNG) to send all illegal migrants to be processed and settled in that country, can be seen as a re-run of the same scenario. It is expected that 'economic refugees' seeking a better life in Australia would certainly be disheartened to be forcibly settled in a tropical Third World country that is no better than where they came from.

This essay attempts an analysis of the Australian perspective on illegal inward migration by sea from South Asia. It excludes illegal migration through air that is comparatively less in numbers.

What is Illegal Migration?

According to the International Organization for Migration (IOM) (2013)[1]—the intergovernmental agency in the field of migration, there is no universally accepted definition for 'migrant' at the international level. The term migrant has been used to include all cases where the decision to migrate has been taken freely by the individual concerned for reasons of 'personal convenience' and without intervention of an external compelling factor. Therefore, it covers persons and family members moving to another country or region to better their material or social life and improve their prospects.

Illegal migration or irregular migration is the movement of people outside the regulatory boundaries of the originating, transit and targeted countries. The IOM estimates that up to 15 percent of the world's total 214 million international migrants are illegal immigrants.

There is no clear or universally accepted definition of irregular migration either. From the standpoint of targeted countries, it is the entry, stay or work in a country without the necessary authorisation or documents required under their immigration regulations. Viewed from the standpoint of the originating country, the irregularity occurs when a person crosses an international boundary without a valid passport or travel document or does not fulfil the administrative requirements for leaving the country. However, the term 'illegal migration' is increasingly used at present times for instances of smuggling migrants across borders or trafficking in persons.

1. Frank Laczko, et al., "Migrant wellbeing and development," International Organization for Migration (IOM) (September 2013), http://publications.iom.int/bookstore/free/WMR2013_EN.pdf.

The United Nations Office on Drugs and Crimes in it's Smuggling of Migrants Protocol defines the smuggling of migrants as "the procurement, in order to obtain, directly or indirectly, a financial or other material benefit, of the illegal entry of a person into a State Party of which the person is not a national or a permanent resident".[2]

In terms of Article 5 of the Protocol, migrants are not liable to criminal prosecution for the fact of having been smuggled. It is therefore understood that the Protocol aims to target smugglers, not the people being smuggled.

Article 6 of the Protocol requires States to criminalise both smuggling of migrants and enabling a person to remain in a country illegally in order to obtain, directly or indirectly, a financial or other material benefit, as well as to establish aggravating circumstances and acts that endanger the lives or safety or entail inhuman or degrading treatment of migrants.

One of the hallmarks of illegal immigration is that it is specifically upward, from poorer countries to the rich countries. The 'push-pull' incentive is the quality of life in the host country compared to the originating country. This is true in the case of South Asian illegal migration to Australia. However, the required payments to smugglers are not so cheap. Because of this, the migrants who choose this path are not from the poorest within the population of the originating countries.

Trafficking in persons involves more complex issues such as international terrorism, people trafficking for prostitution, child abuse, asylum seeking and illegal employment, and so forth.

Studies by Salt and Stein (1997),[3] into the smuggling of migrants have shown that it is an established branch of well-organised 'international gangster syndicate'. The authors have suggested that international migration be treated as a global business that consists of legitimate and illegitimate sides—a business that is run for commercial gain. The core of

2. United Nations, "Protocol against the Smuggling of Migrants by Land, Sea and Air, Supplementing the United Nations Convention against Transnational Organized Crime," *United Nations Office on Drugs and Crime* (2000). https://www.unodc.org/documents/southeastasiaandpacific/2011/04/som-indonesia/convention_smug_eng.pdf.
3. John Salt and Jordan Stein, "Migration as a Business: The Case of Trafficking." *International Migration,* vol. 35, no. 4, 1997, pp. 467–494.

the illegitimate business has been described as the trafficking in persons and smuggling of migrants.

Therefore, the authors recommend that the policymakers need to look at immigration controls in new ways, placing sharper focus on the institutions and vested interests involved in it, rather than on the migrants themselves.

Differences between Trafficking and Smuggling

The differences between trafficking and smuggling are listed below.

Trafficking	Smuggling
Person is recruited using fraud or deception	Person seeks service from smuggler
Legal or illegal border crossing	Illegal border crossing
Legal or illegal documents—withheld from the person	Illegal documents—false or stolen for the person
Controlled—by coercion, threats, fraud or deception	Voluntary—person is not controlled by smuggler
Profit from exploiting victim—ongoing	Profit from moving people—ends at the border
Violation of human rights—exploitation based	Violation of the border—transportation based

Source: New Zealand Government Information campaign to stop people smuggling.

Why Australia?

Australian continent's resource rich, sparsely populated huge land mass and its ever increasing need for skilled and unskilled human resources have made it immensely attractive for new settlers, both regular as well as irregular.

Its history of welcoming 'boat people' in the 1970s has given an erroneous impression, especially to those in South Asia eager to seek greener pastures. Hence, the stream of irregular migrants originating from those regions cannot easily be contained by the respective national authorities. On the other hand, policing to protect and secure a 60,000-km long coastline of Australian land mass is indeed an insurmountable task for Australia.

Australia's Maritime Domains[4]

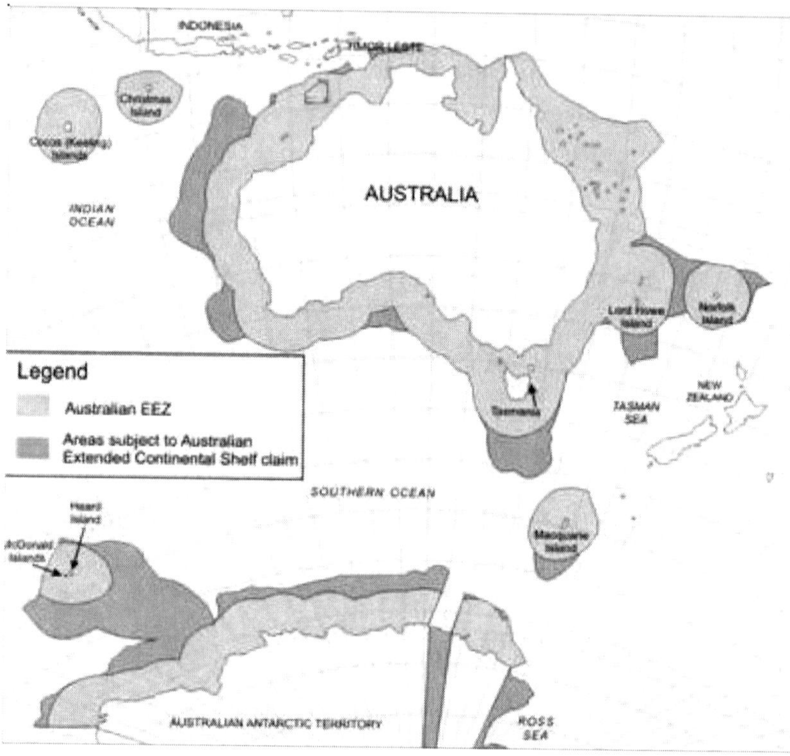

Illegal Migration and Illegal workers

Under the Australian Legal system, those who are allowed to work are Australian citizens, permanent residents and New Zealand citizens only. Foreign nationals intending to work must obtain visas that give permission to work and these visas are given only after very rigorous and prolonged screening process. Any non-Australian citizen working in Australia without a visa or those who are lawfully in Australia but working in breach of visa conditions are classified as 'illegal workers'.

Illegal workers create a lot of problems to the Australian society. They displace those with legitimate rights to work in Australia, Tasmania and New Zealand, and place additional burden on taxpayers in terms of

4. Lee Cordner, "Securing Australia's maritime domain," *Australian Review of Public Affairs, The University of Sydney* (August 2008). http://www.australianreview.net/digest/2008/08/cordner.html.

expenses to locate and remove them and through fraudulently claimed government benefits. Since they would work for lower wages, legal workers may not be able to compete with them. This results in exploitation and paves way for organised criminal activities as well. These illegal workers may not meet the stringent Australian health and character requirements.

The Australian authorities have taken a serious view of these problems and work closely with the community, employers, labour contractors and the industrial sector; a full solution is yet to be found.

The Australia India Institute's March 2013 report 'The Indian Ocean Region: Security, Stability and Sustainability in the 21st Century' includes Australia in the Indian Ocean system in contrast to peripheral regional systems. The report stresses that "to ensure long-term national and regional stability, the maximisation of human security should be a central goal". One of the conclusions of the report is that "there is a need to develop cooperative mechanisms for collectively dealing with displaced persons, refugees and people trafficking".[5]

Australia's National Policy Towards Refugees

Australia has traditionally followed a more humanitarian treatment with regard to illegal immigrants arriving as refugees seeking asylum. The government considered that it has an obligation not to return anybody to a place where they would be prosecuted or subjected to serious harm, such as torture, cruel inhuman or degrading treatment, punishment or arbitrary deprivation of life.

This policy necessitated an assessment of asylum seekers' protection needs. Being aware of this requirement, the smugglers of migrants worked out ways and means to meet the requirement by providing necessary briefings on how to dupe the Australian immigration authorities as part of their human trafficking package.

By the late 1990s, faced with the increasing numbers of irregular migration into Australia, the government had to find new ways of

5. Dennis Rumley, et al., "The Indian Ocean Region: Security, Stability and Sustainability in the 21st Century," *Australia India Institute* (March 2013). www.aii.unimelb.edu.au/file/448/download?token=0SsoKHWU.

conducting these assessments. The method of 'overseas processing' known as the 'Pacific Solution' was mooted by the then Howard Government. It yielded immediate results decreasing the arrivals from 5516 in 2001 to 1 person in 2002.

With the change of government in 2007, policy changes saw the so called 'Pacific Solution' discarded and the illegal boat arrivals picked up and peaked in 2012 to a record high of 17,202. During the seven years of Labour Government, that is, from 2007 to 2013—it has been recorded that a total of 44,465 have arrived by boats or attempted to arrive illegally in Australia.[6]

Figure 7.1: Boat Arrivals by Calendar Year 1979 to 2012 and Financial Year 1989–90 to 2012–13

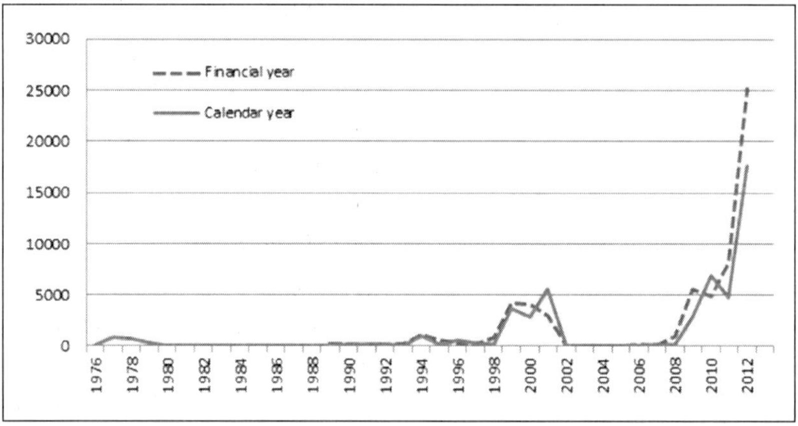

Source: Research Paper by Janet Phillips and Harriet Spinks: published by Social Policy Section, Department of Parliamentary Services, Parliament of Australia, July 2013.

Under Prime Minister Kevin Rudd, Australia is once again gearing up for a general election in Septembers 2013. The hot political issue of 'Boat People' has resurfaced and on July 19, 2013, Rudd declared that all boat people arriving in Australia henceforth, would be sent to PNG, its nearest northern neighbour. Even if the migrants prove they are genuine 'refugees'

---

6. Jannet Phillips and Harriet Spinks, "Boat Arrivals in Australia since 1976," Research Paper, Social Policy Section, Department of Parliamentary Services, Parliament of Australia (July 2013). http://www.aph.gov.au/about_parliament/parliamentary_departments/parliamentary_library/pubs/bn/2012-2013/boatarrivals#_ftn91

they will not be offered a new life in Australia but will be resettled in PNG, one of the poorest pacific countries.

The Costs

The Australian Government's cost associated with irregular migrants arriving by boat, as well as to counter people smuggling efforts are significant, but to arrive at an exact figure is difficult. However, funding for Offshore Asylum Seeker Management in the Department of Immigration and Citizenship (DIAC) is estimated at $2.87 billion for 2013–14 alone. Despite the significant funding which has been provided in recent years for counter-people smuggling activities and deterrence measures, the costs associated with the interception, detention and processing of irregular maritime arrivals remain high. While the full extent of expenditure in this area may never be known, this attempt to identify relevant expenditure reveals that the costs must clearly run into billions of dollars over time.

A glimpse of the enormous cost to the Australian Government is provided in the offshore expenses estimated in the 2013/14 Budget.[7]

Table 7.1: DIAC Funding for Offshore Asylum Seeker Management, 2008–09 to 2013–14

	2008–09 (estimated actual) $m	2009–10 (estimated actual) $m	2010–11 (estimated actual) $m	2011–12 (estimated actual) $m	2012–13 (estimated actual) $m	2013–14 (Budget estimate) $m
Administered expenses						
Community and detention services	35.2	149.4	561.9	780.0	1709.5	2458.1

7. Harriet Spinks, et al., "Australian Government Spending on Irregular Maritime Arrivals and Counter-People Smuggling Activity," Research Paper, Social Policy Section, Department of Parliamentary Services, Parliament of Australia (September 2013). http://www.aph.gov.au/About_Parliament/Parliamentary_Departments/Parliamentary_Library/pubs/rp/rp1314/PeopleSmuggling#_Toc366059599

Management and care of irregular immigrants in Indonesia	-	5.0	3.0	10.0	-	-
Regional cooperation and capacity building	17.0	28.9	32.2	47.2	-	-
Returns and reintegration assistance packages	-	-	5.0	6.9	-	-
Refugee status determinations for offshore entry persons	-	-	-	17.4	-	-
Regional cooperation framework	-	-	-	4.4	-	-
Regional Support Office	-	-	-	0.7	-	-
Departmental expenses	59.2	121.0	160.7	303.8	396.9	409.2
Total administered and departmental expenses for Program 4.3 Offshore Asylum Seeker Management	111.5	304.3	762.8	1170	2106.4	2867.4

Source: Immigration and Citizenship portfolio, Portfolio budget statements 2009–10 onwards.

Note: Departmental expenses include service delivery, policy advice and program design. These are not disaggregated by each administered component of Program 4.3 in the budget papers.

What lies ahead?

The threat of illegal migration to Australia from South Asia cannot be solved unilaterally by Australia alone. The neighbouring New Zealand has so far been relatively safe because of its location in the roaring forties that poses navigational difficulties particularly for the multi-day light fishing vessels used by the smugglers. That does not mean that New Zealand can remain complacent.

Since human smuggling is a multimillion-dollar industry and given correct conditions, the smugglers can use larger vessels that can be stationed in the high seas and launch small boatloads of migrants. It is recalled here that the international terrorist outfit Liberation Tigers of Tamil Eelam stationed 'floating arms warehouses' loaded with weapons and ammunition as well as light aircraft in knocked-down condition and speed boats, and so forth, in the high seas during the height of Sri Lanka's campaign against terrorism.

Recently, the New Zealand Immigration Minister Nathan Guy (2012), introducing the Immigration Amendment Bill to Parliament had this to say:

> It is not only small boats that may be involved, as Canada found out a couple of years ago when a steel-hulled freighter sailing from Thailand was intercepted off the coast of British Columbia with around 500 people on board, all of whom claimed asylum. If people-smugglers can reach Canada, they can certainly reach New Zealand. Our distance and perceived remoteness does not make us immune to such risks. We need to make sure that we properly address and mitigate those risks.[8]

The awareness of the problems inherent in the present day irregular migration at both sides of the Tasman Sea needs to be consolidated and further developed into a common approach. Although the problems confronted in coping up with the stream of irregular migrants have very high economic and political stakes, efforts have to be made to make it a win-win situation.

One sobering factor is that in the long run, South Asia is destined to recover socially and economically that may decrease the demand for people smuggling.

8. New Zealand Parliament Hansard and Journals, Hansard (debates), Vol 679, p. 1950, sitting date 3 May 2012, http://www.parliament.nz/en-nz/pb/debates/debates/50HansD_20120503_00000012/immigration-amendment-bill-%E2%80%94-first-reading.

The 2013 Human Development Report, 'The Rise of the South: Human Progress in a Diverse World', which was launched by United Nations Development Programme's (UNDP) Administrator Helen Clark and Mexican President Enrique Peña Nieto in March 2013, projects a very encouraging picture for developing countries in the South. "The rise of the South is radically reshaping the world of the 21st century, with developing nations driving economic growth, lifting hundreds of millions of people from poverty and propelling billions more into a new global middle class". It further comments that "the rise of the South is unprecedented in its speed and scale" and "never in history have the living conditions and prospects of so many people changed so dramatically and so fast."[9]

The statistics in the report confirm the positive trends which show that "the South as a whole is driving the global economic growth and societal change for the first time in centuries and it is creating opportunities for new partnerships between the South and the North—or developing countries and developed countries, respectively—to confront shared challenges, such as climate change and to cooperate in new ways to speed human development advancement elsewhere in the world."

The challenge posed by the illegal migration from South Asia to Australia and its neighbour New Zealand is an ideal opportunity to strive for such cooperation between the North and South.

Ironically, such views and concepts have been highlighted in the 1994 Human Development Report of UNDP that introduced a new concept of human security, which equates security with people rather than territories, with development rather than arms. It examines both the national and the global concerns of human security.

The report also dealt with these concerns through a new paradigm of sustainable human development, capturing the potential peace dividend, a

9. United Nations Development Programme, "The Rise of the South: Human Progress in a Diverse World," *Human Development Report 2013* (2013). http://hdr.undp.org/sites/default/files/reports/14/hdr2013_en_complete.pdf.

new form of development cooperation and a restructured system of global institutions.[10]

These concepts have buttressed the ideas in the Report of the Commission on Human Security (2003) that human security is "to protect the vital core of all human lives in ways that enhance human freedoms and human fulfilment. Human security means protecting fundamental freedoms—freedoms that are the essence of life. It means protecting people from critical (severe) and pervasive (widespread) threats and situations. It means using processes that build on people's strengths and aspirations. It means creating political, social, environmental, economic, military and cultural systems that together give people the building blocks of survival, livelihood and dignity."[11]

Australia's Foreign and Trade Policy White Paper (2003) stated that "In the globalised 21st century, what is becoming increasingly clear is that the traditional realist model of security—principally embodied in the view that threats emanate from one state, are aimed at another state and are of a military nature–has increasingly come into question.[12]"

Dupont (2003) expressed similar sentiments: "Furthermore, the specific nature of these 'nontraditional' security threats—for example, people smuggling, drug trafficking, piracy and terrorism—require 'nontraditional' response by security agencies."[13]

It appears that, the new security threats in the Indian Ocean Region essentially require a new approach to regional security thinking and cooperation at various levels. Considering the costs committed for the traditional systems that are being exercised by Australia, the detention

10. United Nations Development Programme, *Human Development Report 1994* (March 1994). http://hdr.undp.org/sites/default/files/reports/255/hdr_1994_en_complete_nostats.pdf.
11. United Nations Commission on Human Security, "Human Security Now," *Commission on Human Security,* (2003). http://reliefweb.int/sites/reliefweb.int/files/resources/91BAEEDBA50C6907C1256D19006A9353-chs-security-may03.pdf.
12. Commonwealth of Australia 2003, Advancing the National Interest" Australia's Foreign and Trade Policy White Paper" 2003, http://geneva.mission.gov.au/files/gene/2003_whitepaper.pdf.
13. Alan DuPont, "Transformation or Stagnation? Rethinking Australia's Defence," *Australian Journal of International Affairs,* vol. 57, no. 1, 2003, pp. 55–76.

approach cannot be considered as a sustainable solution. A new approach to address the 'security of people' rather than the 'security of states' could be more fruitful.

As a long-term solution to the illegal migration, Australia needs to rethink about cooperation with the originating countries to uplift the political, social, environmental, economic and cultural systems of the vulnerable groups and actively participate in sustainable effort to obtain enduring results.

In the final analysis, creating collective security and freedom from fear in the Indian Ocean Region requires all regional states to heed to the advice given by the UN Secretary General Kofi Annan (2005) in his report to the UN General Assembly (59th session):

In order to provide effective collective security in the twenty-first century, I urge Heads of State and Government to pledge concerted action against the whole range of threats to international peace and security, and in particular to:

> Affirm and commit themselves to implementing a new security consensus based on the recognition that threats are interlinked, that development, security and human rights are mutually interdependent, that no State can protect itself acting entirely alone and that all States need an equitable, efficient and effective collective security system; and therefore commit themselves to agreeing on, and implementing, comprehensive strategies for confronting the whole range of threats, from international war through weapons of mass destruction, terrorism, State collapse and civil conflict to deadly infectious disease, extreme poverty and the destruction of the environment.[14]

Bibliography

Alan DuPont, "Transformation or Stagnation? Rethinking Australia's Defence," *Australian Journal of International Affairs*, vol. 57, no. 1, 2003.

---

14. Kofi Annan, "In Larger Freedom: Towards Development, Security and Human Rights for All," *United Nations Report of the Secretary General*, Fifty Ninth Session, A/59/2005 (March 2005), http://www.un.org/en/ga/search/view_doc.asp?symbol=A/59/2005.

Commonwealth of Australia 2003, Advancing the National Interest, "Australia's Foreign and Trade Policy White Paper" 2003, http://geneva.mission.gov.au/files/gene/2003_whitepaper.pdf, accessed on September 6, 2015.

Dennis Rumley, et al., "The Indian Ocean Region: Security, Stability and Sustainability in the 21st Century," *Australia India Institute* (March 2013). www.aii.unimelb.edu.au/file/448/download?token=0SsoKHWU, accessed on September 2, 2015.

Frank Laczko, et al., "Migrant wellbeing and development," *International Organisation for Migration (IOM),* (September 2013), http://publications.iom.int/bookstore/free/WMR2013_EN.pdf, accessed on September 3, 2015.

Harriet Spinks, et al., "Australian government spending on irregular maritime arrivals and counter-people smuggling activity," Research Paper, Social Policy Section, Department of Parliamentary Services, Parliament of Australia (September 2013). http://www.aph.gov.au/About_Parliament/Parliamentary_Departments/Parliamentary_Library/pubs/rp/rp1314/PeopleSmuggling#_Toc366059599, accessed on September 8, 2015.

Janet Phillips and Harriet Spinks, "Boat Arrivals in Australia since 1976," Research Paper, Social Policy Section, Department of Parliamentary Services, Parliament of Australia, (July 2013). http://www.aph.gov.au/about_parliament/parliamentary_departments/parliamentary_library/pubs/bn/2012-2013/boatarrivals#_ftn91, accessed on September 8, 2015.

John Salt and Jordan Stein, "Migration as a Business: The Case of Trafficking." *International Migration,* vol. 35, no. 4, 1997.

Kofi Annan, "In Larger Freedom: Towards Development, Security and Human Rights for All," *United Nations Report of the Secretary General,* Fifty Ninth Session, A/59/2005 (March 2005), http://www.un.org/en/ga/search/view_doc.asp?symbol=A/59/2005, accessed on September 3, 2015.

Lee Cordner, "Securing Australia's maritime domain," *Australian Review of Public Affairs, The University of Sydney* (August 2008). http://www.australianreview.net/digest/2008/08/cordner.html, accessed on September 7, 2015.

Nathan Guy, "Immigration Amendment Bill—First Reading," *New Zealand Parliament Hansard (Debates)* [Sitting date: May 3, 2012.], Wellington.

New Zealand Parliament, Hansard and Journals, Hansard (debates), vol. 679, p. 1950, sitting date May 3, 2012.

"The PNG solution—The shadow of looming election falls on desperate asylum seekers," *The Economist,* July 27, 2013, Print edition.

United Nations Commission on Human Security, "Human Security Now," Commission on Human Security, (2003). http://reliefweb.int/sites/reliefweb.int/files/resources/91BAEEDBA50C6907C1256D19006A9353-chs-security-may03.pdf, accessed on September 3, 2015.

United Nations Development Programme, "Human Development Report 1994," *UNDP* (March 1994). http://hdr.undp.org/sites/default/files/reports/255/hdr_1994_en_complete_nostats.pdf, accessed on September 3, 2015.

United Nations Development Programme, "The Rise of the South: Human Progress in a Diverse World," *Human Development Report 2013* (2013). http://hdr.undp.org/sites/default/files/reports/14/hdr2013_en_complete.pdf, accessed on September 1, 2015.

United Nations Office on Drugs and Crime, "A Short Introduction to Migrant Smuggling," *United Nations Office on Drugs and Crime Website* (2010). https://www.unodc.org/

documents/human-trafficking/Migrant-Smuggling/Issue-Papers/Issue_Paper_-_A_short_introduction_to_migrant_smuggling.pdf, accessed on September 7, 2015.

United Nations, "Protocol against the Smuggling of Migrants by Land, Sea and Air, Supplementing the United Nations Convention against Transnational Organized Crime," *United Nations Office on Drugs and Crime,* (2000). https://www.unodc.org/documents/southeastasiaandpacific/2011/04/som-indonesia/convention_smug_eng.pdf, accessed on August 28, 2015.

8. Conclusion

Sithara Fernando

This edited volume is based on the comprehensive maritime security approach. Thus, it takes a broad approach to maritime security. It considers the marine environment, illegal fishing and illegal seaborne migration as maritime security issues. Certainly, states must give due priority to national comprehensive maritime security. However, this volume is also about the Indian Ocean Region (IOR). When one considers the regional context, the transboundary nature of maritime security issues such as the one's identified above becomes obvious. This can put states in something of a dilemma. First and foremost, states must safeguard their national comprehensive maritime security. However, a purely national approach will not always suffice in dealing with transboundary maritime security issues, such as the marine environment, illegal fishing and illegal seaborne migration. One way to resolve this dilemma is by identifying the interests of the states involved with regard to each of these issues and then cooperating on the basis of those interests. Therefore, this conclusion will first attempt to decipher the interests of the states concerned with regard to the marine environment, illegal fishing and illegal seaborne migration from the chapters presented in this volume. Following identification of the interests of the concerned states in each of these issue areas, it will attempt to point out areas for cooperation based on those interests.

Sri Lanka's Interests and the Marine Environment

Chapter 2 by Dr. SinhaRaja Tammita-Delgoda ends with the following words: for an island nation, the preservation of its marine environment transcends issues like conservation, tourism and economics. It is much more than just a cause, it is a fundamental national interest.

This statement clearly establishes the preservation of the marine environment as one of Sri Lanka's most important interests. The sea is crucial to Sri Lanka as an island nation. As Tammita-Delgoda puts it "the sea is Sri Lanka's environment." Regarding the preservation of the marine environment as an interest opens up a range of aligned interests. These include protection of coral reefs, breeding grounds of fish and marine ecosystems in general as well as international cooperation. International cooperation can include international organisations, reaching out to foreign public and foreign private institutions. The most important among these is cooperation with international organisations including the United Nations (UN). The United Nations gives a lot of importance to the preservation of the environment through a range of bodies and instruments. A small country like Sri Lanka has much to gain from cooperation with the United Nations. Another important interest is reaching out to foreign and particularly Western public opinion which is very sensitive to environmental concerns. The image of Sri Lanka in the eyes of foreign public will gain tremendously if it plays a leading role in the preservation of the marine environment. A third aligned interest is cooperation with foreign private institutions that promote the preservation of the environment. In particular, Western private institutions have tremendous financial resources to commit to research on and preservation of the environment. Today, the environment has become an important comprehensive as well as global security concern and Sri Lanka has much to gain from prioritising the preservation of the marine environment as an interest.

Marine Environment and Opportunities for Cooperation

The natural environment in general and the marine environment in particular, are classic cases of transboundary security issues and Chapter 2 by Dr. Tammita-Delgoda shows a sound awareness of this reality. He identifies many opportunities for Sri Lanka to cooperate on the marine environment. First, Tammita-Delgoda advocates that Sri Lanka should become a member of the International Coral Reef Initiative (ICRI). Such a move could contribute tremendously to the preservation of Bar Reef, Sri Lanka's largest marine protected area, a complex of reefs off Kalpitiya Peninsula on the northwestern coast. Second, he recommends that Sri Lanka initiate a programme to study and preserve Dugong, one of the rarest marine mammals on earth. Some of the few remaining places in which Dugong can be found are Sri Lanka's Puttalam and Mannar Lagoons. Because there is a lot of international concern about the preservation of Dugong, Tammita-Delgoda argues that an initiative to preserve Dugong would do much to raise Sri Lanka's standing in the international community. A third opportunity for cooperation identified by Tammita-Delgoda is with the Pew Global Shark Conservation Campaign. The Pew Global Shark Conservation Campaign is an initiative of the Pew Charitable Trust of the United States. This is a viable option for Sri Lanka because it has a large number of sharks in its waters. A fourth cooperative opportunity available for Sri Lanka is with the Caribbean island nation of Bahamas on the preservation of sharks. A fifth opportunity for cooperation on the marine environment available to Sri Lanka is with the International Whaling Commission (IWC) in the preservation of whales. Initiatives to protect the marine environment in cooperation with the international community such as the ones advocated by Tammita-Delgoda can also indirectly help Sri Lanka, as he notes, to bring to its attention the damage being done to Sri Lanka's marine environment by the harmful fishing methods used by Indian trawlers engaging in illegal fishing in Sri Lankan waters. Furthermore, Tammita-Delgoda advocates leveraging of the Indian Ocean Marine Affairs Cooperation (IOMAC) initiative which now functions under Sri Lanka's Ministry of Foreign Affairs and its past work on the marine environment to Sri Lanka's advantage. Finally, he calls on Sri Lanka to venture into the relatively new field of environmental diplomacy in the pursuit of its marine environmental interests.

Sri Lanka's Interests in the Fisheries Sector

Fisheries are an important source of Sri Lanka's national wealth. The fisheries sector also provides livelihoods to many Sri Lankans. In this context, the large-scale illegal fishing engaged in by fishermen from southern India pose a threat to Sri Lanka's fishery resources and the livelihoods of Sri Lankan fishermen. The Indian fishermen are breaching the International Maritime Boundary Line (IMBL) in large numbers and on a regular basis. Sri Lanka's interests in the fisheries sector consist of the following: ensuring maritime border security, protecting fish stocks, safeguarding the livelihoods of Sri Lankan fishermen and prevention of conflict between Sri Lankan and Indian fishermen. With regard to maritime border security in Chapter 3, Cdr. (retired) Lanka Prasada has proposed the installation of Offshore Floating Barriers (OFBs). As pointed out by Prasada, the qualities of OFBs are as follows:

- stop impacts of individual or multiple high speedboats, safely and securely;
- prevent penetration by larger boats at lower speed;
- provide a clearly visible line of demarcation (deterrent effect);
- allow security forces to have a clear field of view through the barrier;
- designed to withstand varying wind, wave and tidal forces;
- availability of built-in gates;
- high resistance to corrosion, ultraviolet degradation, low maintenance requirements/costs;
- fast and cost-effective installation;
- solar-powered lighting can be fixed to the barriers to facilitate identification in the night.

According to Prasada, "the impact-withstand ability of the barriers have been tested through 'Crash Tests' using boats with varying weights and speeds up to 40 knots." Thus, Prasada builds a convincing argument for installation of OFBs along Sri Lanka's IMBL with India. If one goes by Prasada's argument, OFBs could be an effective measure for preventing encroachment of Sri Lanka's maritime border and they could make a valuable contribution to safeguarding its security. A pilot programme could be conducted by the relevant Sri Lankan authorities to test the effectiveness of OFBs. The proposal for installation of OFBs along Sri Lanka's maritime boundary with India is one that should be at least seriously considered by the Sri Lankan government. This is a measure that Sri Lanka can implement independently to safeguard its interest in maritime border security. In addition, Sri Lanka should also take steps to regard protecting fish stocks, safeguarding the livelihoods of Sri Lankan fishermen and prevention of conflict between Sri Lankan and Indian fishermen as maritime interests.

India's Interests in the Fisheries Sector

This section will attempt to decipher India's interests in the fisheries sector. The following are some of the issues facing India's marine fisheries identified by Dr. Prabhkaran Paleri in Chapter 5: declining catches, post-harvest losses, habitat degradation, climate change impact and illegal, unreported and unregulated (IUU) fishing. One could construe India's interests in the fisheries sector from the issues identified by Dr. Paleri. It can be surmised that India is likely to have interests in preserving fish stocks, development of the fisheries industry, preserving marine ecosystems, mitigating and adapting to climate change and combatting IUU fishing. Based on Chapter 4 by Cmde. (retired) R.S. Vasan, the prevention of conflict between Indian fishermen and fishermen of other countries, and international cooperation could also be added to the list of those that are likely to be India's interests in the fisheries sector. For Sri Lanka, it is also important to draw attention to the interests of the Indian state of Tamil Nadu in the fisheries sector. In comparison with the central government of India, Tamil Nadu tends to have a hard-line stance on the fishery issue, often insisting that Tamil Nadu fishermen have a right to fish in the waters off Katchatheevu, an island off the northwestern coast of Sri Lanka. This is because Tamil Nadu tends to oppose the 1974 and 1976 agreements between Sri Lanka and India that recognised the island of Katchatheevu as Sri Lankan territory. Given the hard-line stance of Tamil Nadu in the fisheries sector, it would be far easier for Sri Lanka to deal with the Indian central government on the fisheries issue.

Fisheries Sector and Opportunities for Cooperation

The following are Sri Lanka's interests in the fisheries sector: ensuring maritime border security, protecting fish stocks, safeguarding the livelihoods of Sri Lankan fishermen and prevention of conflict between Sri Lankan and Indian fishermen. India's likely interests in the fisheries sector are the following: preserving fish stocks, development of the fisheries industry, preserving marine ecosystems, mitigating and adapting to climate change, combatting IUU fishing, prevention of conflict between Indian fishermen and fishermen of other countries and international cooperation. It is obvious from the interests of Sri Lanka and the likely interests of India, in the fisheries sector identified above, that there are many common or similar interests. Sri Lanka's interest in maritime border security and India's likely interest in combatting IUU fishing has much similarity. The attainment of both must involve ensuring maritime border security against illegal fishing. Thus, there is scope for Sri Lanka and India to cooperate on maritime border security. Cmde. Vasan in Chapter 4 has proposed joint patrols by Indian and Sri Lankan maritime forces. The interest of Sri Lanka and the likely interest of India in preserving marine fish stocks are identical. However, this interest essentially involves each country preserving its own respective fish stocks. With regard to this interest, there is scope for scientific cooperation on the preservation of fish stocks. There is some similarity in the Sri Lankan interest in safeguarding the livelihoods of Sri Lankan fishermen and the likely Indian interest in the development of the fisheries industry as well. In principle, it can be argued that the development of the fisheries industry would do much to not only safeguard but also improve the livelihoods of fishermen. Therefore, Sri Lanka could take a cue from India's interest in the development of the fisheries industry to develop its own. Possible areas for cooperation here are aquaculture and deep-sea fishing. Sri Lanka's interest in the prevention of conflict between Sri Lankan and Indian fishermen is almost identical with India's interest in preventing conflicts between Indian and foreign fishermen. With regard to this interest, enforcing law and order at sea is an area in which the two countries can cooperate. This section clearly indicates that there are many opportunities for Sri Lanka and India to engage in interest-based cooperation in the fisheries sector.

Sri Lanka's Interests in Combating Illegal Seaborne Migration

In 2013 when this volume was conceptualised, boatloads of illegal migrants were being frequently interdicted by the Sri Lankan Navy (SLN) in the waters off Sri Lanka. The target country for most of these illegal migrants was Australia. These incidents were regularly reported by the Sri Lankan news media. At the time this concluding chapter is being written the flow of illegal migrants from Sri Lanka to Australia has abated somewhat. At this time, the Sri Lankan news media does not report cases of attempted illegal seaborne migration as often. Sri Lanka has taken a great deal of effort and committed substantial resources to prevent illegal migration, both offshore and on land. As indicated in Chapter 6 by Lt. Col. Saman Jayawickrama, Sri Lanka's interests in combating the threat posed by illegal seaborne migration are to ensure the security of its maritime border and to prevent the trafficking of wanted terrorists across its maritime border. It has been reported that the pro-Liberation Tigers of Tamil Elam outfits, which continue to be active, have been involved in human smuggling. Not only can these outfits smuggle wanted terrorists across Sri Lanka's borders but also smuggle ordinary people into Australia and extort money from them to fund their activities. Therefore, illegal migration has both short and long-term consequences for Sri Lanka's national security and it is a threat against which Sri Lanka must continue to be vigilant.

Australia's Interests in Combatting Illegal Seaborne Migration

In Chapter 7, Mr. Ananda Weerasinghe and Mr. Mahinda Attanayake provide an analysis of Australia's response to illegal seaborne migration from South Asia to Australia. This concluding chapter will use their work to decipher Australia's likely interests with regard to the threat posed by illegal seaborne migration from South Asia. First, one can safely surmise that in the post-9/11 age, Australia is likely to have an interest in preventing terrorists from breaching its maritime border and entering its territory. Australia is also likely to have an interest in preventing illegal migrants in general from entering its territory. This would entail a related and very important interest in maritime border security. The entry of illegal migrants into Australia would be detrimental to its domestic law and order because illegal migrants are likely to engage in illegal activities.

Opportunities for Cooperation in Combatting Illegal Seaborne Migration

The following are Sri Lanka's interests in combating the threat posed by illegal seaborne migration: ensuring the security of its maritime border and preventing the trafficking of wanted terrorists across its maritime border.

The following are Australia's likely interests in combating this threat: preventing terrorists from breaching its maritime border and entering its territory, preventing illegal migrants in general from entering its territory and ensuring its maritime border security. The interests of Sri Lanka and Australia in combating illegal seaborne migration listed above indicate that as responsible states, they share a lot of common ground on this issue. First and foremost, both states have an interest in ensuring the security of their respective maritime borders. While the threat of illegal seaborne migration appears to have abated somewhat at the time of writing this conclusion, the two countries should take action to ensure that it does not arise again in the future. For Sri Lanka, at an operational level, this involves strengthening the capacity of its navy to patrol the maritime border. In 2013, Australia gifted two Bay-class patrol boats to Sri Lanka for countering the threat of illegal seaborne migration. Such initiatives can do much to strengthen the capacity of the Sri Lanka Navy (SLN) to ensure the security of its maritime border. On this issue based on their identical interests in ensuring the security of their respective maritime borders, a bilateral cooperative option available to the two states is to open up a regular channel of communication between the two navies aimed at ensuring that the threat does not arise again in the future. Another cooperative option open to them is to put in place a mechanism for intelligence cooperation aimed at remaining vigilant about this threat. Sri Lanka's interest in ensuring that wanted terrorists do not breach its maritime border from the inside and Australia's interest in ensuring that wanted terrorists do not breach its maritime border from the outside also has a great deal of complementarity. At the time of writing this conclusion, the Islamic State has magnified manifold the threat that terrorism has been posing to the world since 9/11. The Islamic State is in the close vicinity of the Indian Ocean Region (IOR). With the Western powers strengthening their offensive against the Islamic State, to borrow an argument put forward by 'The Economist' in the wake of the horrendous series of terrorist attacks in Paris in November 2015 for which the Islamic State claimed responsibility, Western cities might become 'soft targets' for terrorist attacks by the

Islamic State.[1] Australia is a member of the Western alliance and Islamic State terrorists could use the maritime route of the Indian Ocean to infiltrate into Australia, and Sri Lanka's geographic location close to the centre of the Indian Ocean could make it vulnerable as a transit point in that route. The likelihood of Islamic State terrorists utilising criminal networks that promote illegal seaborne migration or human smuggling entails that efforts to combat this threat must be given a high degree of importance within the comprehensive maritime security approach. When one takes together the complementarity of Sri Lanka's and Australia's interests in preventing the movement of terrorists, a possible increase in the vulnerability of Australian cities to Islamic State terrorist attacks, the vulnerability of Sri Lanka to exploitation as a transit point, cooperation in the tracking of terrorist movements and joint action in apprehending them become crucial areas in which Sri Lanka and Australia could engage in interest-based cooperation. The defence and law enforcement agencies of the two countries should give serious consideration to such an initiative given the heightening of the terrorist threat posed by the Islamic State.

This edited volume has been an interesting academic exercise in exploring the contours of comprehensive maritime security. Essentially, the state and maritime forces are providers of comprehensive maritime security. At the same time, maritime security should not be limited to military affairs alone. The sustained attention given to the deterioration of the marine environment, illegal fishing and illegal seaborne migration in this volume has convincingly demonstrated the security threats they can pose to both states and people. This volume has been an exercise in validating the comprehensive maritime security approach. It has also demonstrated that when one considers comprehensive maritime security in a regional context such as the Indian Ocean Region (IOR) the transboundary nature of threats such as the deterioration of the marine environment, illegal fishing and illegal seaborne migration is put into sharp relief. States should and must take independent action to safeguard their national

1. "Why France and Why Now?" *The Economist*, November 15, 2015. http://www.economist.com/news/middle-east-and-africa/21678518-recent-spate-attacks-islamic-state-suggests-jihadists-are-changing-tactics-what, accessed on November 18, 2015.

comprehensive maritime security. In several places this concluding chapter has highlighted the independent actions Sri Lanka can take to ensure its national comprehensive maritime security. For example, with regard to illegal fishing, it has highlighted Cdr. Lanka Prasada's proposal to put in place Offshore Floating Barriers (OFBs), and with regard to illegal seaborne migration, it has called for strengthening the capacity of the Sri Lanka Navy (SLN) to patrol the maritime border. At the same time, given the transboundary nature of the threats to comprehensive maritime security discussed in this volume, independent action taken by individual states might not always be enough. In order to resolve the dilemma posed for the state by transboundary maritime threats, this volume has proposed interest-based cooperation. This concluding chapter has made an effort to decipher Sri Lanka's interests with regard to the marine environment, Sri Lanka's interests and India's likely interests in the fisheries sector, and Sri Lanka's interests and Australia's likely interests in combating illegal seaborne migration. Based on the identified interests or likely interests, it has proposed a number of areas in which these countries can engage in interest-based cooperation. The purpose of interest-based cooperation is to ensure national comprehensive maritime security. The regional context of the IOR indicates that both independent and collaborative efforts are needed to ensure national comprehensive maritime security.

Furthermore, it can be argued that the model of interest-based cooperation espoused here could be extended to the regional level of the IOR to address the transboundary maritime threats, such as illegal fishing and illegal seaborne migration. Admittedly, multilateral interest-based cooperation would be more difficult than bilateral interest-based cooperation advocated in this concluding chapter because of the greater number of states involved. But the fact of the matter is that often multilateral cooperation initiatives once they are formally institutionalised, develop agendas of their own to the detriment of the interests of the participating states. Interstate multilateral cooperation can face difficulties when this happens. At a time when the Indian Ocean Rim Association (IORA) is just beginning to establish itself as the widely recognised multilateral organisation in the IOR, both the IORA and the regional community of states would do well to pay some heed to the interest-based cooperation approach in order to facilitate smoother regional cooperation in the long run on transboundary maritime threats, such as illegal fishing and illegal seaborne migration.

Bibliography

"Why France and Why Now?" *The Economist*, November 15, 2015. http://www.economist.com/news/middle-east-and-africa/21678518-recent-spate-attacks-islamic-state-suggests-jihadists-are-changing-tactics-what, accessed on November 18, 2015.

Index